Family Violence

DISCARD

Other Books in the Current Controversies Series

Family Violence

Dedria Bryfonski, Book Editor

GREENHAVEN PRESS
A part of Gale, Cengage Learning

GALE
CENGAGE Learning·

Detroit • New York • San Francisco • New Haven, Conn • Waterville, Maine • London

GALE
CENGAGE Learning·

Elizabeth Des Chenes, *Director, Publishing Solutions*

© 2013 Greenhaven Press, a part of Gale, Cengage Learning

Gale and Greenhaven Press are registered trademarks used herein under license.

For more information, contact:
Greenhaven Press
27500 Drake Rd.
Farmington Hills, MI 48331-3535
Or you can visit our Internet site at gale.cengage.com

For product information and technology assistance, contact us at

Gale Customer Support, 1-800-877-4253
For permission to use material from this text or product, submit all requests online at www.cengage.com/permissions

Further permissions questions can be emailed to permissionrequest@cengage.com

Articles in Greenhaven Press anthologies are often edited for length to meet page requirements. In addition, original titles of these works are changed to clearly present the main thesis and to explicitly indicate the author's opinion. Every effort is made to ensure that Greenhaven Press accurately reflects the original intent of the authors. Every effort has been made to trace the owners of copyrighted material.

Cover image ejwhite/ShutterStock.com.

LIBRARY OF CONGRESS CATALOGING-IN-PUBLICATION DATA

Family violence / Dedria Bryfonski, book editor.
   p. cm. -- (Current controversies)
Includes bibliographical references and index.
   ISBN 978-0-7377-6225-9 (hardcover) -- ISBN 978-0-7377-6226-6 (pbk.)
  1. Family violence. I. Bryfonski, Dedria.
  HV6626.F3296 2012
  362.82'92--dc23

                                2012023470

Printed in the United States of America
1 2 3 4 5   16 15 14 13 12

FD277

Contents

Chapter 1: What Contributes to Family Violence?

Research in Canada shows different patterns for men and women with a history of being abused as a child. Women are more likely to have emotional and psychological disorders and to attempt suicide, whereas men are more likely to abuse alcohol.

Gender-Based Violence Is a Special Problem for African American Women

Tricia B. Bent-Goodley

While gender-based violence is a global problem, African American women are especially at risk. They are more likely to suffer severe forms of violence and less likely to receive treatment.

No: Family Violence Is Not a Gender Issue

Family Violence Is a Human Problem, Not a Gender Problem

John Hamel

The latest research shows that men and women initiate domestic violence at very similar rates. Although men suffer fewer physical injuries, men and women suffer emotional injuries in equal proportions.

Women Are as Likely as Men to Abuse a Partner

Murray A. Straus

Numerous studies have shown that men and women have the same risk factors for intimate partner abuse and that both sexes, in fact, abuse partners at approximately the same rates. These facts have been concealed from the public by researchers with a feminist agenda.

Lesbians Are Not Immune to Abusive Relationships

Victoria A. Brownworth

Reports of intimate partner violence are increasing at an alarming rate among young women, and women in lesbian relationships—despite cultural stereotypes—are almost as likely to be victims as their heterosexual counterparts.

Chapter 3: Are Efforts to Reduce Family Violence Effective?

Yes: Efforts to Reduce Family Violence Are Effective

Traditional methods of dealing with family violence, such as restraining orders, have been only marginally effective. The Scarlet Letter proposal shows a promising new approach. Under this proposal, a registry of domestic abusers would be made available on the Internet, enabling people to avoid or be more wary of known batterers.

No: Efforts to Reduce Family Violence Are Not Effective

Chapter 4: What Are the Consequences of Family Violence?

A study of teens at high risk for substance abuse revealed that exposure to violence in the home increased the risk of alcohol abuse in early adulthood for girls but not for boys. Exposure to family violence had no impact on drug abuse in early adulthood for either sex, according to the study.

Child Welfare Information Gateway

Many victims of child abuse and neglect suffer physical consequences such as impaired brain development and poor physical health, psychological consequences such as psychiatric disorders and cognitive difficulties, and behavioral consequences such as juvenile delinquency and substance abuse. There are additional consequences to society as a whole in the form of direct costs such as those associated with the child welfare system and indirect costs due to such factors as unemployment.

Foreword

By definition, controversies are "discussions of questions in which opposing opinions clash" (*Webster's Twentieth Century Dictionary Unabridged*). Few would deny that controversies are a pervasive part of the human condition and exist on virtually every level of human enterprise. Controversies transpire between individuals and among groups, within nations and between nations. Controversies supply the grist necessary for progress by providing challenges and challengers to the status quo. They also create atmospheres where strife and warfare can flourish. A world without controversies would be a peaceful world; but it also would be, by and large, static and prosaic.

The Series' Purpose

The purpose of the Current Controversies series is to explore many of the social, political, and economic controversies dominating the national and international scenes today. Titles selected for inclusion in the series are highly focused and specific. For example, from the larger category of criminal justice, Current Controversies deals with specific topics such as police brutality, gun control, white collar crime, and others. The debates in Current Controversies also are presented in a useful, timeless fashion. Articles and book excerpts included in each title are selected if they contribute valuable, long-range ideas to the overall debate. And wherever possible, current information is enhanced with historical documents and other relevant materials. Thus, while individual titles are current in focus, every effort is made to ensure that they will not become quickly outdated. Books in the Current Controversies series will remain important resources for librarians, teachers, and students for many years.

In addition to keeping the titles focused and specific, great care is taken in the editorial format of each book in the series. Book introductions and chapter prefaces are offered to provide background material for readers. Chapters are organized around several key questions that are answered with diverse opinions representing all points on the political spectrum. Materials in each chapter include opinions in which authors clearly disagree as well as alternative opinions in which authors may agree on a broader issue but disagree on the possible solutions. In this way, the content of each volume in Current Controversies mirrors the mosaic of opinions encountered in society. Readers will quickly realize that there are many viable answers to these complex issues. By questioning each author's conclusions, students and casual readers can begin to develop the critical thinking skills so important to evaluating opinionated material.

Current Controversies is also ideal for controlled research. Each anthology in the series is composed of primary sources taken from a wide gamut of informational categories including periodicals, newspapers, books, US and foreign government documents, and the publications of private and public organizations. Readers will find factual support for reports, debates, and research papers covering all areas of important issues. In addition, an annotated table of contents, an index, a book and periodical bibliography, and a list of organizations to contact are included in each book to expedite further research.

Perhaps more than ever before in history, people are confronted with diverse and contradictory information. During the Persian Gulf War, for example, the public was not only treated to minute-to-minute coverage of the war, it was also inundated with critiques of the coverage and countless analyses of the factors motivating US involvement. Being able to sort through the plethora of opinions accompanying today's major issues, and to draw one's own conclusions, can be a complicated and frustrating struggle. It is the editors' hope that Current Controversies will help readers with this struggle.

Introduction

> *"Many believe that there is an epidemic of family violence occurring today in the United States."*

The untimely death of singer Whitney Houston in February 2012 became an occasion for the rehashing of tales of her stormy fifteen-year marriage to singer Bobby Brown, a marriage marked by numerous episodes of domestic violence. In a notable incident in 2003, police responding to a 911 call found Houston with a bruised cheek and cut lip. Brown was charged with misdemeanor battery as a result of the incident.

In 1986, Oprah Winfrey surprised her viewers when she revealed during a television show on sexual abuse that she herself was a victim. While her mother was working long hours as a maid, Winfrey was left with family members in the inner-city apartment in Milwaukee that she shared with her mother. A cousin, uncle, and family friend repeatedly molested her from the ages of 9 to 13, Winfrey claimed.

In October 2009, Anthony Marshall, the eighty-five-year-old son of socialite and philanthropist Brooke Astor, was convicted of fourteen charges involving stealing from his mother. In addition to defrauding his mentally incompetent mother (who had died in 2007 at age 105), Marshall had made her do without amenities and medical attention: He fired devoted staff, refused to take her to doctor's appointments, and failed to refill prescriptions.

These three high-profile stories represent a small sample of the millions of cases of family violence taking place each year in the United States. *Family violence* is an umbrella term encompassing abuse occurring within the family unit. Some of the most common forms are intimate partner abuse, child abuse, and elder abuse. Many believe that there is an epidemic of family violence occurring today in America. Certainly, the statistics are alarming.

- According to a November 2011 survey by the Division of Violence Prevention of the federal Centers for Disease Control and Prevention, nearly three out of every ten women and one out of every ten men in the United States have experienced rape, physical violence, or stalking by an intimate partner.

- The US Department of Health and Human Services reports that 3.3 million allegations of child abuse were made in 2010, affecting approximately 6 million children.

- Two million Americans aged sixty-five or older have been victims of abuse or neglect by their caregivers, with 60 percent of the perpetrators of abuse being family members, according to the National Center on Elder Abuse.

The family is the primary social group of the human community, traditionally assumed to provide a safe, loving environment in which children are nurtured by parents. Sadly, this is not always the case. Among family members many individuals experience intimate partner abuse; physical, sexual, or emotional abuse as children; and financial, physical, or emotional abuse as elders.

English common law held that women were inferior to men and that wives were the property of their husbands. Early marriage laws permitted husbands to hit their wives. In fact, the term *rule of thumb* is said to refer to the commonly accepted rule that the thickness of the stick that men were allowed to use in beating their wives could be no larger than the thickness of the man's thumb.

In the United States, the first stirrings of the women's movement began in the mid-1800s. The Seneca Falls Convention of 1848 declared that "all men and women are created equal," and it protested the common belief that husbands have the right to physically punish their wives. The sentiments expressed by these early feminists attracted little attention. In 1976, however, when the National Organization for Women (NOW) decided to make wife-battering a priority issue, violence against women received significant attention. Two milestones were achieved in 1978: the formation of the National Coalition Against Sexual Assault and the National Coalition Against Domestic Violence. Another milestone was achieved on September 13, 1994, when the federal Violence Against Women Act was signed into law.

Historically, children were regarded as the property of their parents and were often subjected to economic exploitation, including being sent to work at an early age to help the family or being abandoned because their care created an additional economic hardship that poor families could not bear. Child abuse was first recognized as a problem in the late 1800s, resulting in the passage of some child-protection laws in the early 1900s.

In 1962, child abuse was recognized as a serious problem. The landmark article "The Battered Child Syndrome" by C. Henry Kempe and colleagues, which appeared in the *Journal of the American Medical Association*, defined child abuse as a medical problem. Kempe led efforts to enact legislation protecting children, and within ten years every US state had begun requiring medical and educational professionals to report suspected child abuse to the police. In 1974, the Child Abuse Prevention and Treatment Act was passed, funding programs to help individuals identify and report child abuse and to provide shelter and other protective services to victims.

The maltreatment of the elderly was acknowledged in ancient times. In 44 BC, Cicero, the Roman philosopher and statesman, spoke of the plight of older people: "Old age will only be respected if it fights for itself, maintains its rights, avoids dependence on anyone, and asserts control over its own to its last breath." Nonetheless, through the following centuries, abuse of the elderly remained mostly a hidden problem. The passage of the Older Americans Act in 1973 laid the groundwork for most of the federal programs in the United States aimed at protecting the rights of older Americans. In 1974, the passage of Title XX of the Social Security Act gave permission to states to use Social Services Block Grant funds for the protection of adults.

G.R. Burston drew attention to the issue of elder abuse in a September 6, 1975, letter to the editors of the *British Medical Journal* titled "Granny Battering," in which he stated, "Hardly a week goes by without some reference in the national press or medical journals to baby battering, and I think it is time that all of us realized that elderly people too are at times also battered." However, it was not until the late 1980s and early 1990s that elder abuse was recognized as a serious problem. A milestone in addressing problems of elder abuse was the 1989 establishment of the National Association of Adult Protective Services.

Family violence and its impact on society are hotly contested issues. The viewpoints of various professionals on these issues are here presented under the following chapters headings: What Contributes to Family Violence?, Is Family Violence a Gender Issue?, Are Efforts to Reduce Family Violence Effective?, and What Are the Consequences of Family Violence?

CHAPTER 1

What Contributes to Family Violence?

Overview: The Causes of Intimate Partner Violence

National Institute of Justice

The National Institute of Justice is the research, development, and evaluation agency of the US Department of Justice.

Research supported by NIJ [National Institute of Justice] and others has identified some of the causes of, and risk factors for, intimate partner violence (often called "domestic violence"). Intimate partner violence has serious physical, psychological, economic, and social consequences.

- One in five women killed or severely injured by an intimate partner had *no warning*: the fatal or life-threatening incident was the first physical violence they had experienced from their partner. A woman's attempt to leave an abuser was the precipitating factor in 45 percent of the murders of women by their intimate partners.

- *Early parenthood* is a risk factor. Women who had children by age 21 were twice as likely to be victims of intimate partner violence as women who were not mothers at that age. Men who had fathered children by age 21 were more than three times as likely to be abusers as men who were not fathers at that age.

- Although alcohol is not the cause of violence against women, a significant relationship exists between male perpetrator *problem drinking* and violence against intimate female partners. Severe drinking problems increase the risk for lethal and violent victimization of women in intimate partner relationships. More than two-thirds of the offenders who commit or attempt homicide used alcohol, drugs, or both during the incident; less than one-fourth of the victims did.

- *Severe poverty* and its associated stressors increase the risk for intimate partner violence—the lower the household income, the higher the reported intimate partner violence rates. Moreover, researchers found that reductions in benefits from Aid to Families with Dependent Children (AFDC) were associated with an increase in intimate partner homicides.

- Intimate partner violence is *linked with unemployment*; one study found that intimate partner violence impairs a woman's capacity to find employment. Another study of women who received AFDC benefits found that domestic violence was associated with a general pattern of reduced stability of employment.

- Women who have experienced serious abuse face overwhelming *mental and emotional distress*. Almost half of the women reporting serious domestic violence also meet the criteria for major depression; 24 percent suffer from posttraumatic stress disorder, and 31 percent from anxiety.

Substance Abuse and Intimate Partner Violence Are Strongly Connected

Elaine Zahnd, May Aydin, David Grant, and Sue Holtby

Elaine Zahnd is a senior research scientist at the Public Health Institute, in Oakland, California; May Aydin is a research and survey support manager at the UCLA Center for Health Policy Research; David Grant is the California Health Information Survey director at the UCLA Center for Health Policy Research; and Sue Holtby is a program director at the Public Health Institute.

In 2009, an estimated 3.5 million California adults ages 18–65 reported that they had been a victim of physical and/or sexual intimate partner violence [IPV] since age 18 (14.8%). Furthermore, nearly one-quarter of California adults who experienced IPV reported an incident occurring in the previous 12 months (24.1%). And nearly 82,000 adults in California (8.4%) indicated they were victims of a recent sexual IPV incident. Women were more than twice as likely as men to have been a victim (20.5% vs. 9.1%); overall, almost 2.5 million women had experienced adult IPV.

Unlike many injuries, the physical and sexual scars of IPV may have lingering consequences on the mental health [MH] and health behaviors of its victims. Many adult IPV victims appear reluctant to discuss their experiences with others, including criminal justice authorities, friends, family members, health care providers or counselors. Lack of disclosure can compound the trauma of IPV and result in decreased coping and increased anxiety, depression or other emotional health issues for the adult victim.

Elaine Zahnd, May Aydin, David Grant, and Sue Holtby, "The Link Between Intimate Partner Violence, Substance Abuse, and Mental Health in California," *Health Policy Brief*, UCLA Center for Health Policy Research, August 2011, pp. 1–6. All rights reserved. Reproduced by permission.

Less apparent is whether there is any lingering psychological effect from long past but not forgotten IPV incidents. And although studies suggest an association between alcohol use and IPV, little is known about the extent of substance-related IPV or its effect on emotional health.

Using data from the 2009 California Health Interview Survey (CHIS 2009), this policy brief illustrates how IPV impacts victims' emotional health, their use of substances, and their need for and utilization of mental health (MH) or alcohol and other drug services in California.

More Psychological Distress

Among the 3.5 million Californians who have been victims of adult IPV, over half a million (594,000) reported symptoms in the past year associated with serious psychological distress [SPD], which includes the most serious kinds of diagnosable mental health disorders, such as anxiety and depression. Victims of adult IPV were also more than three times as likely as unexposed adults to have reported past-year SPD (16.8% vs. 5.3%, respectively). Among victims of recent IPV, nearly 172,000 reported symptoms of SPD (21.6%) during the past year, a higher rate than among adults who have not had a recent IPV incident (16%).

For women who experienced adult IPV, 17.5% reported SPD in the past year compared to 5.9% of women who have never been IPV victims. Male adult IPV victims were also more likely to experience SPD compared to non-victims, with 15.3% reporting past-year psychological distress versus only 4.7% of male non-victims. While there are not significant differences by gender among adult IPV victims for past-year psychological distress (17.5% vs. 15.3%), larger numbers of female victims are affected by SPD (428,000) than male victims (166,000) since women make up the majority of IPV cases.

Violence-Related Substance Abuse

While alcohol or other drugs [AOD] do not directly cause IPV, they may increase the risk of violent incidents in households where IPV has occurred in the past. Alcohol and other drugs may also play a role in escalating the frequency and severity of IPV incidents.

More than half of all IPV victims subjected to a recent incident (52.4%) report engaging in binge drinking over the past year.

When asked if their partner appeared to be drinking alcohol or using drugs during the most recent violent incident, almost half (47.6%) replied in the affirmative. Women were significantly more likely to report that their partner was using alcohol or other drugs during the most recent IPV incident compared to men (49.6% vs. 29.4%).

Alcohol may also be consumed by victims in an attempt to cope with the emotional and/or physical pain associated with violence. Adult IPV victims were more likely to report binge drinking in the past year (39%) than those who have never been a victim of IPV (34.2%).

More than half of all IPV victims subjected to a recent incident (52.4%) report engaging in binge drinking over the past year, a significantly higher rate than those who have not experienced a recent IPV incident (35.1%). And 7% of recent IPV victims reported daily to weekly binge drinking, a level higher than that among those never exposed to IPV (4.5%).

Nearly one in three adults who reported being an adult IPV victim said they needed help for a mental or emotional, or alcohol or other drug problem (33.1%). In contrast, just 12.6% of non-victims in California noted needing similar help. And 39.9% of adults who recently experienced an IPV incident expressed a need for emotional health or AOD counseling, services or treatment compared to 30.3% among those adult IPV victims who did not have a recent IPV incident.

No gender differences among victims of adult IPV emerged, with both female victims (33.6%) and male victims (31.9%) acknowledging a similar need for help. When victims are compared to non-victims by gender, among women, adult IPV victims were more than twice as likely to express a need for emotional or AOD help than non-victims (33.6% vs. 14.5%). Regarding men, 31.9% of adult IPV victims said that they needed assistance for MH or AOD problems compared to just 10.9% of non-victims.

More than 2.7 million Californians reported seeing a health care provider or therapist for emotional or mental health and/or for alcohol or other drug issues in the past year (11.6%). Of these, adult IPV victims were 2.5 times more likely than non-victims to report seeing their primary care physician, a psychiatrist, social worker or counselor in the past year for problems with their psychological or emotional health and/or use of alcohol or other drugs (23.9% vs. 9.5%).

Female victims of adult IPV were more likely than male victims to report visiting a general practitioner, mental health or AOD professional for counseling or treatment in the past year (26.2% vs. 18.7%). Female victims of adult IPV were also more than twice as likely to report mental health or AOD visits during the past year (26.2%) compared to female non-victims (11.4%). The male pattern was similar: 18.7% of male adult IPV victims had such visits compared with only 7.9% of non-victims.

In 2009, over 3.5 million Californians said they were adult IPV victims and of those, over half a million reported experiencing symptoms associated with serious psychological distress. While it is understandable that recent IPV incidents would have a strong association with feelings of poorer emotional health, what seems notable from these findings is that Californians who have been victimized by an intimate partner—often years earlier—reported past year symptoms of SPD at higher rates than those never exposed to IPV. Although SPD is due to multiple causes, it appears likely that harboring emotional feelings from long-past IPV victimization may be influential. IPV victims are also more likely to express a need for mental health or AOD services at significantly higher levels than non-victims. Similarly, victims of adult IPV are visiting primary care doctors, social workers and other counselors for emotional health, alcohol or other drug problems at often twice the rate as non-victims of adult IPV.

Strong Connections

These findings also reveal strong connections between IPV and substance use. Victims report high levels of partner AOD involvement during the most recent incident. Women are more likely to report that their partners were using alcohol or other drugs during the most recent incident compared to men. In the aftermath of violence, some victims may turn to alcohol, perhaps as self-medication to cope with or mask their pain.

The associated risk factors identified in this brief appear to have the greatest impact on women. While male victims suffer much of the same trauma and may seek out similar coping strategies as females, the sheer number of female Californians affected is noteworthy.

Several policy changes and interventions can help protect and aid in the healing of adults subjected to IPV. There continues to be a critical need for additional mental health, substance use and domestic violence services. According to the Substance Abuse and Mental Health Services Administration, national spending on mental health and substance abuse account for a decreasing share of health care spending. Despite passage of a national mental health parity law, a recent survey indicates that only 10% of Americans have heard of the law and almost half do not know if their insurance would cover mental health services (45%). And although the California budget was recently passed, additional mental health, AOD and domestic violence program cuts are still possible if future revenues do not materialize.

Expanding Screening

Health screening for IPV, for emotional health, and for substance use problems among patients/clients, regardless of gender, should be expanded, standardized and made routine. Medical doctors and other health care providers can be proactive by screening and referring IPV victims with emotional health and AOD problems to appropriate services. Mental health and substance abuse counselors should also initiate IPV screening and, if needed, referrals for counseling, shelters and legal advice. Counselors of IPV victims need to routinely screen for mental health and AOD concerns among victims.

Finally, public health messages about the links between IPV, mental health and substance abuse can raise awareness and foster outreach to those who may need medical, IPV, AOD and mental health services.

Honor Killings Are Caused by Extreme Cultural and Religious Beliefs

Phyllis Chesler

Phyllis Chesler is emerita professor of psychology and women's studies at City University of New York. She is the author of numerous books, including Women and Madness.

To combat the epidemic of honor killings requires understanding what makes these murders unique. They differ from plain and psychopathic homicides, serial killings, crimes of passion, revenge killings, and domestic violence. Their motivation is different and based on codes of morality and behavior that typify some cultures, often reinforced by fundamentalist religious dictates. In 2000, the United Nations [U.N.] estimated that there are 5,000 honor killings every year. That number might be reasonable for Pakistan alone, but worldwide the numbers are much greater. In 2002 and again in 2004, the U.N. brought a resolution to end honor killings and other honor-related crimes. In 2004, at a meeting in The Hague about the rising tide of honor killings in Europe, law enforcement officers from the U.K. [United Kingdom] announced plans to begin reopening old cases to see if certain murders were, indeed, honor murders. The number of honor killings is routinely underestimated, and most estimates are little more than guesses that vary widely. Definitive or reliable worldwide estimates of honor killing incidence do not exist.

Most honor killings are not classified as such, are rarely prosecuted, or when prosecuted in the Muslim world, result in relatively light sentences. When an honor killing occurs in the

Phyllis Chesler, "Worldwide Trends in Honor Killings," *Middle East Quarterly*, v. 17, no. 2, Spring 2010, p. 3. All rights reserved. Reproduced by permission.

West, many people, including the police, still shy away from calling it an honor killing. In the West, both Islamist and feminist groups, including domestic violence activists, continue to insist that honor killings are a form of Western-style domestic violence or femicide (killing of women). They are not. This study documents that there are at least two types of honor killings and two victim populations. Both types differ significantly from each other, just as they differ from Western domestic femicide. One group has an average age of seventeen; the other group's average age is thirty-six. The age difference is a statistically significant one.

Families Killing Their Young Women

The study's findings indicate that honor killings accelerated significantly in a 20-year period between 1989 and 2009. This may mean that honor killings are genuinely escalating, perhaps as a function of jihadist [pertaining to Muslim holy war] extremism and Islamic fundamentalism, or that honor killings are being more accurately reported and prosecuted, especially in the West, but also in the East. The expansion of the Internet may account for wider reporting of these incidents.

The worldwide average age of victims for the entire population is twenty-three. This is true for all geographical regions. Thus, wherever an honor killing is committed, it is primarily a crime against young people. Just over half of these victims were daughters and sisters; about a quarter were wives and girlfriends of the perpetrators. The remainder included mothers, aunts, nieces, cousins, uncles, or non-relatives. Honor killings are a family collaboration. Worldwide, two-thirds of the victims were killed by their families of origin. Murder by the family of origin was at its highest (72 percent) in the Muslim world and at its lowest in North America (49 percent); European families of origin were involved almost as often as those in the Muslim world, possibly because so many are first- or second-generation immigrants and, therefore, still tightly bound to their native cultures. Alternatively, this might be due to the Islamist radicalization of third or even fourth generations. Internationally, fathers played an active role in over one-third of the honor murders. Fathers were most involved in North America (52 percent) and least involved in the Muslim world; in Europe, fathers were involved in more than one-third of the murders.

Worldwide, 58 percent of the victims were murdered for being "too Western."

Worldwide, 42 percent of these murders were carried out by multiple perpetrators, a characteristic which distinguishes them considerably from Western domestic femicide. A small number of the murders worldwide involved more than one victim. Multiple murders were at their highest in North America and at their lowest in Europe. In the Muslim world, just under a quarter of the murders involved more than one victim. Additional victims included the dead woman's children, boyfriend, fiance, husband, sister, brother, or parents.

Worldwide, more than half the victims were tortured; i.e., they did not die instantly but in agony. In North America, over one-third of the victims were tortured; in Europe, two-thirds were tortured; in the Muslim world, half were tortured. Torturous deaths include: being raped or gang-raped before being killed; being strangled or bludgeoned to death; being stabbed many times (10 to 40 times); being stoned or burned to death; being beheaded, or having one's throat slashed.

Finally, worldwide, 58 percent of the victims were murdered for being "too Western" and/or for resisting or disobeying cultural and religious expectations. The accusation of being "too Western" was the exact language used by the perpetrator or perpetrators. Being "too Western" meant being seen as too independent, not subservient enough, refusing to wear varieties of Islamic clothing (including forms of the veil), wanting an advanced education and a career, having non-Muslim (or non-Sikh or non-Hindu) friends or boy-friends, refusing to marry one's first cousin, wanting to choose one's own husband, choosing a socially "inferior" or non-Muslim (or non-Sikh or non-Hindu) husband; or leaving an abusive husband. There were statistically significant regional differences for this motive. For example, in North America, 91 percent of victims were murdered for being "too Western" as compared to a smaller but still substantial number (71 percent) in Europe. In comparison, only 43 percent of victims were killed for this reason in the Muslim world.

Less than half (42 percent) of the victims worldwide were murdered for committing an alleged "sexual impropriety"; this refers to victims who had been raped, were allegedly having extra-marital affairs, or who were viewed as "promiscuous" (even where this might not refer to actual sexual promiscuity or even sexual activity). However, in the Muslim world, 57 percent of victims were murdered for this motive as compared to 29 percent in Europe and a small number (9 percent) in North America.

Worldwide, younger-age victims were killed by their families of origin 81 percent of the time.

What the Age Differences Mean

This study documents that there are at least two different kinds of honor killings and/or two different victim populations: one made up of female children and young women whose average age is seventeen, the other composed of women whose average age is thirty-six. Both kinds of honor murders differ from Western domestic femicide.

In the non-immigrant West, serious domestic violence exists which includes incest, child abuse, marital rape, marital battering, marital stalking, and marital post-battering femicide. However, there is no cultural pattern of fathers specifically targeting or murdering their teenage or young adult daughters, nor do families of origin participate in planning, perpetrating, justifying, and valorizing such murders. Clearly, these characteristics define the classic honor killing of younger women and girls.

The honor murders of older women might seem to resemble Western-style domestic femicide. The victim is an older married woman, usually a mother, who is often killed by her husband but also by multiple perpetrators (30 percent of the time). Worldwide, almost half (44 percent) of those who kill older-age victims include members of either the victim's family of origin or members of her husband's family of origin. This is extremely rare in a Western domestic femicide; the husband who kills his wife in the West is rarely assisted by members of his family of origin or by his in-laws.

However, in the Muslim world, older-age honor killing victims are murdered by their own families of origin nearly two-thirds of the time. This suggests that the old-world custom has changed somewhat in Europe where the victim's family of origin participates in her murder only one-third (31 percent) of the time. Thus far, in North America, no members of the family of origin have participated in the honor killing of an older-age victim. Whether North America will eventually come to resemble Europe or even the Muslim world remains to be seen, as this will be influenced by immigration and other demographic factors. Finally, nearly half the older-age victims are subjected to a torturous death. However, the torture rate was at its highest (68 percent) in Europe for female victims of all ages. The torture rate was 35 percent and 51 percent in North America and in the Muslim world, respectively.

Worldwide, younger-age victims were killed by their families of origin 81 percent of the time. In North America, 94 percent were killed by their family of origin; this figure was 77 percent in Europe and 82 percent in the Muslim world. In North America, fathers had a hands-on role in 100 percent of the cases when the daughter was eighteen-years-old or younger. Worldwide, younger-age women and girls were tortured 53 percent of the time; however, in Europe, they were tortured between 72 and 83 percent of the time—significantly more than older-age women worldwide.

Western Responses to Honor Killing

Many Western feminists and advocates for victims of domestic violence have confused Western domestic violence or domestic femicide (the two are different) with the honor killings of older-age victims. Representatives of Islamist pressure groups including Council on American-Islamic Relations (CAIR) and the Canadian Islamic Congress, various academics (e.g., Ajay Nair, Tom Keil), activists (e.g., Rana Husseini), and religious leaders (e.g., Abdulhai Patel of the Canadian Council of Imams) have insisted that honor killings either do not exist or have nothing to do with Islam; that they are cultural, tribal, pre-Islamic customs, and that, in any event, domestic violence exists everywhere. Feminists who work with the victims of domestic violence have seen so much violence against women that they are uncomfortable singling out one group of perpetrators, especially an immigrant or Muslim group. However, Western domestic femicide differs significantly from honor killing.

Former National Organization for Women (NOW) president Kim Gandy compared the battered and beheaded Aasiya Hassan to the battered (but still living) pop star Rihanna and further questioned whether Hassan's murder was an honor killing:

Is a Muslim man in Buffalo more likely to kill his wife than a Catholic man in Buffalo? A Jewish man in Buffalo? I don't know the answer to that, but I know that there is plenty of violence to go around—and that the long and sordid history of oppressing women in the name of religion surely includes Islam, but is not limited to Islam.

At the time of the Hassan beheading, a coalition of domestic violence workers sent an (unpublished) letter to the Erie County district attorney's office and to some media stating that this was not an honor killing, that honor killings had nothing to do with Islam, and that sensationalizing Muslim domestic violence was not only racist but also served to render invisible the much larger incidence of both domestic violence and domestic femicide. They have a point, but they also miss the point, namely, that apples are not oranges and that honor killings are not the same as Western domestic femicides.

Honor Killings Reflect Culture

One might argue that the stated murder motive of being "too Westernized" may, in a sense, overlap substantively with the stated and unstated motives involved in Western domestic femicide. In both instances, the woman is expected to live with male violence and to remain silent about it. She is not supposed to leave—or to leave with the children or any other male "property." However, the need to keep a woman isolated, subordinate, fearful, and dependent through the use of violence does not reflect a Western cultural or religious value; rather, it reflects the individual, psychological pathology of the Western batterer-murderer. On the other hand, an honor killing reflects the culture's values aimed at regulating female behavior—values that the family, including the victim's family, is expected to enforce and uphold.

Further, such cultural, ethnic, or tribal values are not often condemned by the major religious and political leaders in developing Muslim countries or in immigrant communities in the West. On the contrary, such communities maintain an enforced silence on all matters of religious, cultural, or communal "sensitivity." Today, such leaders (and their many followers) often tempt, shame, or force Muslim girls and women into wearing a variety of body coverings including the hijab (head covering), burqa, or chadari (full-body covering) as an expression of religiosity and cultural pride or as an expression of symbolic resistance to the non-Muslim West. Muslim men are allowed to dress like Westerners, and no one challenges the ubiquitous use of Western technology, including airplanes, cell phones, the Internet, or satellite television as un-Islamic. But Muslim women are expected to bear the burden of upholding these ancient and allegedly religious customs of gender apartheid.

Frightening honor murders may constitute an object lesson to other Muslim girls and women.

It is clear that Muslim girls and women are murdered for honor in both the West and the East when they refuse to wear the hijab or choose to wear it improperly. In addition, they are killed for behaving in accepted Western or modern ways when they express a desire to attend college, have careers, live independent lives, have non-Muslim friends (including boyfriends with whom they may or may not be sexually involved), choose their own husbands, refuse to marry their first cousins, or want to leave an abusive husband. This "Westernization" trend also exists in Muslim countries but to a lesser extent. Allegations of unacceptable "Westernization" accounted for 44 percent of honor murders in the Muslim world as compared to 71 percent in Europe and 91 percent in North America.

Tempted by Western ideas, desiring to assimilate, and hoping to escape lives of subordination, those girls and women who exercise their option to be Western are killed—at early ages and in particularly gruesome ways. Frightening honor murders may constitute an object lesson to other Muslim girls and women about what may happen to them if they act on the temptation to do more than serve their fathers and brothers as domestic servants, marry their first cousin, and breed as many children as possible. The deaths of females already living in the West may also be intended as lessons for other female immigrants who are expected to lead subordinate and segregated lives amid the temptations and privileges of freedom. This is especially true in Europe where large Muslim ghettos have formed in the past few decades. It is particularly alarming to note that in Europe 96 percent of the honor killing perpetrators are Muslims.

Primal, Sadistic, Barbaric Savagery

The level of primal, sadistic, or barbaric savagery shown in honor killings towards a female family intimate more closely approximates some of the murders in the West perpetrated by serial killers against prostitutes or randomly selected women. It also suggests that gender separatism, the devaluation of girls and women, normalized child abuse, including arranged child marriages of both boys and girls, sexual repression, misogyny (sometimes inspired by misogynist interpretations of the Qur'an), and the demands made by an increase in the violent ideology of jihad all lead to murderous levels of aggression towards girls and women. One only has to kill a few girls and women to keep the others in line. Honor killings are, in a sense, a form of domestic terrorism, meant to ensure that Muslim women wear the Islamic veil, have Muslim babies, and mingle only with other Muslims.

Since Muslim immigration and, therefore, family networks are more restricted in North America than in Europe, honor-killing fathers may feel that the entire burden for upholding standards for female behavior falls heavily upon them and them alone. This may account for the fact that fathers are responsible 100 percent of the time for the honor murders of the youngest-age victims. In Europe and in the Muslim world, that burden may more easily be shared by sons and brothers, grandfathers, uncles, and male cousins.

How can this problem be addressed? Immigration, law enforcement, and religious authorities must all be included in education, prevention, and prosecution efforts in the matter of honor killings.

Western judicial systems and governments have recently begun to address [honor killings].

In addition, shelters for battered Muslim girls and women should be established and multilingual staff appropriately trained in the facts about honor killings. For example, young Muslim girls are frequently lured back home by their mothers. When a shelter resident receives such a phone call, the staff must immediately go on high alert. The equivalent of a federal witness protection program for the intended targets of honor killings should be created; England has already established such a program. Extended safe surrogate family networks must be created to replace existing family networks; the intended victims themselves, with enormous assistance, may become each other's "sisters."

In addition, clear government warnings must be issued to Muslim, Sikh, and Hindu immigrants and citizens: Honor killings must be prosecuted in the West, and perpetrators, accomplices, and enablers must all be prosecuted. Participating families should be publicly shamed. Criminals must be deported after they have served their sentences.

Western judicial systems and governments have recently begun to address this problem. In 2006, a Danish court convicted nine members of a clan for the honor murder of Ghazala Khan. In 2009, a German court sentenced a father to life in prison for having ordered his son to murder his sister for the family honor while the 20-year-old son was sentenced to nine and a half years. In another case, a British court, with the help of testimony from the victim's mother and fiance, convicted a father of a 10-year-old honor murder after the crime was reclassified; and, for the first time, the Canadian government informed new immigrants:

> Canada's openness and generosity do not extend to barbaric cultural practices that tolerate spousal abuse, "honour killings," female genital mutilation or other gender-based violence. Those guilty of these crimes are severely punished under Canada's criminal laws.

Islamic gender apartheid is a human rights violation and cannot be justified in the name of cultural relativism, tolerance, anti-racism, diversity, or political correctness. As long as Islamist groups continue to deny, minimize, or obfuscate the problem, and government and police officials accept their inaccurate versions of reality, women will continue to be killed for honor in the West.

The battle for women's rights is central to the battle for Europe and for Western values. It is a necessary part of true democracy, along with freedom of religion, tolerance for homosexuals, and freedom of dissent. Here, then, is exactly where the greatest battle of the twenty-first century is joined.

There Is a Connection Between Bullying and Domestic Violence

Paul J. Fink

Paul J. Fink is a consultant and psychiatrist in Bala-Cynwyd, Pennsylvania, and a professor of psychiatry at Temple University in Philadelphia.

Bullying and domestic violence have been considered in practice and in the literature as "unconnected phenomena," according to sociologists Kenneth Corvo . . . and Ellen deLara. . . . However, as a clinician, I see a clear continuum between the two.

In my experience, boys who are big and powerful learn to use their power early and find it to be pleasurable. Becoming dominant is important for these boys in school, sports, and social settings, and those who are less powerful tend to fall into line as followers. Shaming and humiliating a weaker boy makes the bully feel highly regarded. We see the learning pattern take place in schools across the country: "I am a winner, and I need to win." Youngsters are under pressure to succeed at home and at school, so the pressure is on them to demonstrate prowess.

Rarely do we meet a family or parents who spend time cataloging their son's failures. It's all about winning! The child hears his father talking about his son's success on the basketball court, his fabulous grades, and so on, and he learns at a very early age what is important to the parent and how to measure himself.

Paul J. Fink, "A Literature Review Seeks to Determine Whether Bullying Is a Risk Factor for Domestic Violence. Do You Think That Bullying and Domestic Violence Are on a Continuum?," *Clinical Psychiatry News*, v. 39, no. 9, September 2011, p. 8. All rights reserved. Reproduced by permission.

The child who is bullied has seriously damaged self-esteem and does little to put himself forward. Clinically, we see a similar process occur in marriage. I have never seen a couple in psychotherapy where each person isn't blaming the other, finding fault with the other, and wanting either retribution or an apology.

A man who deals with frustration by hitting his opponent will be the fellow who commits domestic violence.

Men who beat or injure their wives have the same psychological needs as those of the bully. They, too, need to win, dominate, and in many cases, overpower. They bring these ideas to the marriage from their family home, school, ball field, and workplace.

In America, 3–10 million incidents of domestic violence are reported annually, hundreds of shelters for abused women exist across the country, and thousands of social workers are helping these women and their children. But the problem is not with the women, although many do stay in the relationship and are reportedly further abused. Usually, men—and the way in which they are socialized—are the problem.

If the man is the boss at work, he needs to remain in that role in the house. He cannot tolerate losing an argument or being denied sex or perceive any other "threat" to his authority. If, on the other hand, the husband has no power at work, feels like he is pushed around by everyone, and is low on the totem pole, he comes home looking for some outlet for his frustrated power.

The issue apparently underlying most marital difficulties revolves around control. Who is in charge? Who makes the decisions? In many marriages, there is a frustration of dreams and expectations. A man who deals with frustration by hitting his opponent will be the fellow who commits domestic violence.

I was once consulted by a couple in the days before couples lived together before marriage. They had a great wedding and flew off to their honeymoon. The husband had come from a family of six children whose mother got up every day at 6 a.m. and made a big breakfast for everybody. The wife had grown up in a small apartment where everyone fought over the one bathroom and flew out of the house with cups of coffee in their hands.

On their first day at home, the husband sat at the kitchen table with a knife and fork waiting for his breakfast. He felt a breeze go by as his wife flew out of the apartment with her coffee. That's how it began. They agreed that the honeymoon had been wonderful, but each of them had an idea of what they wanted or expected, and the frustrations, hurts, and disappointments had accumulated by the time they asked for help because of his violent outbursts. All clinicians have heard such stories.

Was the Husband a Bully as a Boy?

Too often, we fail to explore whether the husband had been a bully as a boy. Was he regularly beaten by his father when his behavior was bad? To test out the concept of whether male aggressive behavior is on a continuum, we have to work collectively to get the data. One small study examined three issues shared by men who use violence in their intimate relationships. Those issues are "being part of a family culture that promoted violence, being part of a nonfamily culture that promoted violence; and early experiences of maltreatment or trauma." We also must acknowledge that men, too, are victims of domestic violence. But this phenomenon is far less common.

In some couples, each partner figures out how to frustrate the other. While still proposing love, the need to hurt takes precedence. In a similar fashion, the school bully plans his attack before he even starts out for school. Almost every adolescent arrested has the word "assault" among the charges brought to the court. It seems to start early, and I have for many years thought that we would reduce youth violence and youth murder if we could reduce the fighting, hitting, and hurting that takes place in second, third, and fourth grade.

When we take a close look at bullying, we see that these perpetrators often were victims themselves.

Some boys don't even learn to talk to peers about issues or problems. Similarly husbands don't talk to their wives when they are frustrated or unhappy. I believe the feelings precede the hitting and hurting of their wives. We often ask why they can't just sit down and discuss the issue with their wives. And what I hear is that they blame the woman who "doesn't listen to them," "thinks she is always right," and so on. The wife's chatter, which always contains some criticisms of the husband as far as he's concerned, further infuriates him. Often, that chatter triggers the first punch.

We do not need blood tests or MRIs to understand what leads to bullying and domestic violence. They are related. Inherent in this connection is the training the boy gets in developing anger and hatred. Children who are brutalized in their homes are very angry about it. They need love; instead, they get hurt. Their response is to hurt others. They are filled with anger toward a parent—to whom they cannot retaliate. So the boy's career as a bully starts.

Bullying is always related to a power differential, just like a big daddy and a little son. They have to find someone smaller and weaker who won't retaliate. The bullying continues for many years. In violent relationships in which the two people get married, the man is all set for domestic violence and marital rape. When we take a close look at bullying, we see that these perpetrators often were victims themselves.

A study of middle and high school students in Massachusetts in 2009 found that the adjusted odds ratios for middle school students being physically hurt by a family member were 2.9 for victims, 4.4 for bullies, and 5 for bully-victims. For witnessing violence in the family, those ratios were 2.6, 2.9 and 3.9, respectively, after adjustment for potential difference by age group, sex, and race/ethnicity.

For high school students being physically hurt by a family member, the ratios were 2.8 for victims, 3.8 for bullies, and 5.8 for bully-victims, and for witnessing violence in the family 2.3, 2.7, and 6.8, respectively. "As schools and health departments continue to address the problem of bullying and its consequences, an understanding of the broad range of associated risk factors is important for creating successful prevention and intervention strategies that include involvement by families," the authors wrote.

Safe Schools Initiative Report

These associations between getting bullied and becoming a bully also were found several years ago, in a comprehensive report undertaken by the U.S. Secret Service and the U.S. Department of Education ("The Final Report and Findings of the Safe School Initiative: Implications for the Prevention of School Attacks in the United States"). The report, described as "the culmination of an extensive examination of 37 incidents of targeted school violence that occurred in the United States from December 1974 through May 2000," found that "almost three-quarters of the attackers (in the school shootings) felt persecuted, bullied, threatened, attacked, or injured by others prior to the incident." In fact, the report says that many of the attackers in the school shootings "told of behaviors that, if they occurred within the workplace, likely would meet legal definitions of harassment and/or assault."

We need to help a child feel included and loved, not dominated. We must show that "real men" don't have to win every battle. A man has to come away with a feeling of some power, some ability to succeed, because if he doesn't, he will lose self-esteem, feel worthless, and get depressed.

I've seen numerous older men who come into psycho-therapy with feelings of defeat. These are men who have lived lives of great success, and now the world is passing them by. All the things that used to matter are no longer exciting or available to them. For them, the relative loss of power is ex-cruciatingly painful. They feel that no one understands them. These men are beyond domestic violence, but the underlying factors and needs are still burning within them.

The battering of women for centuries was seen as an ac-ceptable form of behavior that supported patriarchy. Thank-fully—in contemporary America—we vilify domestic violence and its perpetrators. But despite the perpetrator's shame and regret, too often, he cannot stop. Psychological factors drive him to continue his behavior. We must be aware that in every home where domestic violence occurs, the child who wit-nesses or hears it is traumatized.

Aggression as a Modality

Aggression is a modality that has to change. First, parents worldwide have to stop beating their children. Second, I sup-port a nationwide campaign to stop bullying in schools. Fi-nally, we have to get couples to talk before they get married. Such conversations will bring out aggressive tendencies held by either partner and lead to discussions about the changes needed for the pair to have a successful and respectful mar-riage.

A Recessionary Economy Can Increase the Risk of Domestic Violence

Sabrina Rubin Erdely

Sabrina Rubin Erdely, feature writer and investigative journalist, is a contributing editor at Rolling Stone, *a contributing writer at* Philadelphia, *and the author of articles appearing in various other publications.*

Mary Clemons cowered in her sister-in-law's bedroom closet, practically afraid to breathe. She'd known her husband, Chuck (not his real name), would come looking for her sooner or later, and now he'd finally arrived. "Have you heard from her?" Mary heard Chuck demand of his sister, who feigned ignorance. In reality, Mary had been hiding out there for two days, ever since Chuck had smothered her with a pillow until she'd seen spots. Mary had fled their apartment in the middle of the night, leaving their sleeping 3-year-old daughter behind, vowing never to go back. She'd spent the previous couple of days figuring out what to do next.

Now, from the darkness of the closet, 22-year-old Mary listened as Chuck began to cry. "I don't know where she is," he wept to his sister. "I'm so worried." The sound of Chuck's sobbing gave Mary satisfaction—but also flooded her with sympathy. He sounded so miserable. Mary was flattered to realize how devastated Chuck was by her leaving; it was proof that he really did care. She returned home the next day.

"Yep, I went back for more," she says dryly, 20 years later. It wouldn't be the last time. Over her 15-year marriage to

Sabrina Rubin Erdely, "'Why I Finally Left': Like Many Victims of Domestic Abuse, Mary Clemons Escaped. And Then Returned—Many, Many Times. A Report of Why It Can Take So Long to Break Free, and What Every Woman Can Learn from Mary's Experience," *Good Housekeeping*, v. 252, no. 3, March 23, 2011, p. 148. All rights reserved. Reproduced by permission.

Chuck, Mary Clemons fled again and again, with each return plunging her into more horrifying abuse. "Let's see: I've been gagged, tied up, and beaten. Stripped naked in the woods, and chased with a car," remembers Mary, 42, her lilting voice tinged with the twang of her adopted hometown of Terrell, TX. "I've had guns pulled on me, and knives held to my throat. The abuse got pretty wicked." And yet, despite the violence—which was so extreme that a shelter worker once warned her, "On a danger-level scale of one to 10, you're an 11"—she kept going back. Only on her eighth attempt did she finally escape for good, in 2002, at age 33.

Though it might seem inconceivable that a battered woman would keep returning to the person causing her pain, Mary's pattern is utterly typical. Studies have shown that two-thirds of battered women who leave their abusers go back within a year or two; it takes the average survivor five tries before she escapes for good. "Leaving this kind of relationship is a process, because of the huge influence the abuser has on the victim," says Veronique Valliere, . . . a clinical psychologist in Fogelsville, PA, who specializes in treating abuse victims and perpetrators. "She can't just pick up and leave; the abuser makes that impossible by the control he exerts over her life." There's only one way most women can get out of this kind of relationship, says Sheryl Cates, the former CEO of the Texas Council on Family Violence, and that's with outside help. "I would say the vast majority of women who leave do it only with the support of family or friends," Cates asserts.

Financial Stress Can Lead to Abuse

One in four women is abused in her lifetime, and there are 4.8 million intimate-partner-related physical assaults and rapes reported each year, reports the National Violence Against Women Survey, sponsored by the National Institute of Justice and the Centers for Disease Control and Prevention. That makes domestic violence the leading cause of injury to women.

On average, more than three American women are killed by their partners every day, and one-third of all women murdered in the U.S. lose their lives due to domestic abuse, say Department of Justice statistics. And because the economic downturn has contributed to a spike in domestic violence, knowing how to be there for an abused friend is more crucial than ever.

"Without the people who helped me, I'd never have gotten out, and I'd be dead now."

"The economy plays a huge role," says Sue Else, president of the National Network to End Domestic Violence (NNEDV). "When money is tight, when people are anxious about finances, when someone has been laid off, that tension can get funneled into physical abuse." A recent Mary Kay Inc. study found that after the financial markets tanked in September 2008, three out of four domestic violence shelters nationwide saw an increase in women seeking help, with 75 percent of those shelters attributing the surge to "financial issues." Cates concurs, noting that calls to Texas hotlines have jumped as much as 21 percent. However, the sad truth is that shelters have been hit hard by the economic downturn, too: Forty-one percent of them have had to decrease their services, reported a Mary Kay survey released last May, and 88 percent feared that their ability to provide services would stay the same or worsen over the year ahead.

This landscape is undoubtedly discouraging to victims of domestic violence trying to make their escape. And it showcases exactly why a supportive inner circle can make such a huge difference. "Without the people who helped me, I'd never have gotten out, and I'd be dead now," Mary says. She has a survivor's grit, but it's buoyed by a sunny optimism—because when she most needed help, she discovered not only a well-spring of inner strength, but also the courage and compassion of her friends. Together, these allowed her to reinvent her life.

Men Exposed to Political Violence Are More Likely to Be Abusive

Cari Jo Clark et al.

Cari Jo Clark is an assistant professor at the University of Minnesota Medical School.

Collective violence, such as war, state repression, torture, and violent political conflicts, increases risk of various forms of gender-based violence. UN Security Council Resolution 1325 calls for protection of women and girls from such violence in conflict settings. Humanitarian guidelines have been developed to address this issue; however, such guidelines frequently focus on gender-based violence perpetrated by individuals outside the family, often with a particular emphasis on sexual violence. This focus neglects the potentially heightened risk of other forms of gender-based violence to which women might be more exposed, such as intimate-partner violence. Anecdotal evidence suggests that perpetration of intimate-partner violence might increase during episodes of collective violence and its aftermath. Collective and intimate-partner violence have well documented mental and physical health consequences, and exposure to both might raise the risk of deleterious health consequences attributable to cumulative effects of exposure to many traumas. Hence, further examination of the relation between these types of violence is warranted.

Empirical research about the association between collective violence and intimate-partner violence has mainly been of

Cari Jo Clark, et al., "Association Between Exposure to Political Violence and Intimate-Partner Violence in the Occupied Palestinian Territory: A Cross-Sectional Study," reprinted from *The Lancet*, v. 375, no. 9711, January 23, 2010, pp. 310–16. Copyright 2010, with permission from Elsevier.

military personnel. Prevalence estimates for perpetration of physical intimate-partner violence are up to three times higher for veterans and active-duty servicemen than for the general population. For military personnel, exposure to war-zone stressors has been associated with perpetration of intimate-partner violence, a relation that is largely mediated by the presence of post-traumatic stress disorder. Few studies have investigated the link between intimate-partner violence and forms of collective violence in civilian populations, but evidence mostly supports this association.

Exposure to Violent Conflict

Results of studies undertaken in Sri Lanka, Afghanistan, Lebanon, and the West Bank showed that exposure to violent conflict was associated with intimate-partner violence and other forms of domestic violence. In a recent study of immigrant men attending health clinics in Boston, MA, USA, men who reported exposure to preimmigration political violence had much higher rates of past-year perpetration for both physical and sexual intimate-partner violence than did those who were not exposed to such violence. By contrast, results of a multi-country study of women affected by violent conflict showed no association between collective and intimate-partner violence, or an inverse association, dependent on the setting. Limitations of these studies were the study methods used, including an inability to ascertain temporality, non-representative or immigrant population samples; poor response rates; or an absence of adjustment for potential confounding factors. Our analysis attempted to overcome many of these shortcomings.

2005 was a time of political turmoil, instability, and continuing violence in the occupied Palestinian territory. Although Israeli settlements in the Gaza Strip ceased with Israeli disengagement, the West Bank continued to host several hundred thousand settlers. Occupation policies restricting movement of Palestinian people and goods were a defining factor of everyday life, and negatively affected the Palestinian economy. The economic situation in the occupied territory was characterised by widespread poverty and increasing need for development assistance. Exposures to these factors represent forms of political violence that directly (eg, injury and death) and indirectly (eg, economic ramification of policies restricting movement of goods and people) affect human security. Within this context of sustained insecurity, we assessed whether exposure to political violence was associated with increased risk of male-to-female intimate-partner violence on the basis of reports of presently married women.

Overall, 719 (20%) respondents reported personal exposure or exposure of a household or close family member [to violence].

Domestic Violence in Occupied Palestine

A cross-sectional national survey of domestic violence was undertaken by the Palestinian Central Bureau of Statistics (PCBS) in the occupied Palestinian territory between December, 2005, and January, 2006. Population projections based on the 1997 Population, Housing, and Establishment census were used to estimate the Palestinian population in 2005. To achieve a representative sample, PCBS selected a stratified random sample of 234 enumeration areas used in the census. Eighteen households were systematically selected from every area with maps compiled by PCBS, resulting in a sample of 4212 households, of which 4156 participated (99% response).

Within every household, eligible participants were ever-married women aged 15–64 years, unmarried women aged 18 years and older, and women and men older than 65 years. We restricted this analysis to ever-married respondents because intimate relations in Palestinian culture typically take place only within a marital relationship. Of the 3815 ever-married women identified for the study, 3787 participated (3774 completed and 13 partly completed interviews). We restricted our analysis to presently married women because demographic information was available for their husbands; of these participants, we analysed data only from those with complete information for variables of interest (92% participation). . . .

1299 (37%) [of the female] respondents reported no [intimate-partner] violence, 1302 (37%) psychological violence, 538 (15%) physical (but not sexual) violence, 371 (11%) sexual violence only. Overall, women reporting intimate-partner violence were more likely to be younger, less educated, and more likely to live in the West Bank than were those not reporting such violence. Additionally, their husbands were younger and less educated than were husbands of those not reporting violence. Association of this type of violence with employment status and locality (urban, rural, or refugee camp) differed by violence type. . . .

289 (8%) respondents reported that their husbands were directly exposed to political violence. Being insulted or cursed was most frequently reported and being made a fugitive (ie, being sought by Israeli military forces for alleged political, military, or civil resistance against Israel) the least frequently reported. Overall, 719 (20%) respondents reported personal exposure or exposure of a household or close family member. Of family exposure, home break-ins were most frequent and the respondent being arrested was least frequent. Almost half of respondents reported that their household was negatively financially affected by occupation. . . .

Respondents whose husbands were directly exposed to political violence had 47% higher odds of reporting psychological violence only, 89% for physical violence, and 123% for sexual violence compared with those whose husbands were not personally exposed to political violence. Women whose husbands were indirectly exposed through exposure of their family had 61% increased odds of reporting physical intimate-partner violence and 97% for sexual violence compared with those whose husbands were not indirectly exposed to political violence. Reported psychological violence was not associated with indirect exposure of husbands. . . .

Financially Affected Respondents

Respondents whose households were financially affected by measures taken by the occupying forces were 40% more likely to report psychological violence, 51% to report physical violence, and 55% to report sexual violence compared with those whose households were not financially affected. When all three political violence exposures were modelled together, the findings were similar. . . . Association between economic effects of political violence and intimate-partner violence were present in the Gaza Strip but not the West Bank. In the Gaza Strip, women whose households were financially affected by the occupation were at 139% increased odds of reporting psychological intimate-partner violence, 93% for physical violence, and 83% for sexual violence compared with those whose households were not financially affected. No differences by region were identified for exposure of husbands or families to political violence. . . .

We have shown that exposure to political violence is associated with increased odds of psychological, physical, and sexual intimate-partner violence in a sample of presently married women in the occupied Palestinian territory. Our findings are consistent with those from other studies, including research from the occupied Palestinian territory. Results of survey research of Palestinian adolescents has shown associations between exposure to political violence and reports of spousal, child, and sibling abuse. In previous bivariate [showing the relationship between two variables] analyses with variables consisting of the economic effect measure used in our analysis, researchers identified associations between both the husband's job loss and deterioration of the economic situation of the household with psychological, physical, and sexual intimate-partner violence. These findings raise the issue of how political violence might contribute to violence towards intimate partners. Results of research in the occupied Palestinian territory have shown the relevance of integration of several theoretical perspectives to explain the occurrence of such violence.

The Feminist Perspective

The feminist perspective is relevant to understanding the occurrence of intimate-partner violence because patriarchal ideologies and institutional practices underpin violence against women. Pre-existing gender inequalities are exacerbated and traditional gender roles are challenged in environments in which forms of collective violence persist. Occupation policies and interactions with occupation forces entail continuous humiliation for men and renders them unable to protect and provide for their families, potentially leading to frustration and violence against people with less power—namely, women and children. From a resource-theory perspective, violence might be used to reassert men's socially established position of power in the family. . . .

Investigation is needed into the potential pathways leading from political to intimate-partner violence.

Exposure to political violence, its attendant economic consequences, and mobility constraints also negatively affect family functioning and increase household stress and interpersonal conflict, which are risk factors for intimate-partner violence. Intense financial stress is noteworthy, and the economic situation in the Gaza Strip, which is worse than that in the West Bank, could account for the significant association between economic effects of exposure to political violence and intimate-partner violence in Gaza only. Occupation policies, including a separation barrier that is being erected in various parts of the West Bank, affect family connectedness, depriving women of regular contact with their families who might otherwise intervene to prevent intimate-partner violence.

Finally, from a social learning perspective, exposure to violence in childhood is a risk factor for future perpetration of intimate-partner violence. In a study of Palestinian men, researchers reported an increased risk of perpetration of intimate-partner violence associated with childhood exposure to family violence. Results of other research have shown a raised risk of perpetration of child abuse associated with exposure to political violence. Hence, family violence is both cyclical and intertwined with political violence, creating a vicious cycle. . . .

The relation we have shown between intimate-partner violence and exposure to political violence draws attention to the wide-ranging ramifications of political violence towards women and men. Investigation is needed into the potential pathways leading from political to intimate-partner violence, taking into account a range of explanations and their interactions, because any one explanation is insufficient to explain the relation. Our findings also suggest the importance of assessment of different types of violence exposures when considering potential need for psychosocial interventions, since exposure to many traumatic events is associated with increased mental and physical health symptoms. Finally, our findings reinforce the relevance of UN Security Council Resolution 1325—especially the call for all parties to the conflict to protect women and girls from violence and to respect international law.

Is Family Violence a Gender Issue?

Chapter Preface

In February 2009, romantically involved popular singers Chris Brown and Rihanna were in a car when she read a text message from a former girlfriend on his cell phone. Rihanna related the incident to Diane Sawyer on *Good Morning America*:

> I caught him in a lie, and he wouldn't tell the truth. And I wouldn't drop it.... I couldn't take that he kept lying to me, and he couldn't take that I wouldn't drop it.... It escalated into him being violent towards me. And it was ugly.... I was battered, I was bleeding, I was swollen in my face.

Rihanna's injuries were severe enough to require hospitalization. Brown eventually pleaded guilty to criminal assault and was sentenced to probation and community service.

The altercation involving two celebrities received significant media attention and put a spotlight on the issue of domestic violence. The incident also served to perpetuate one of the frequent gender stereotypes of domestic violence: most frequently the male is the aggressor. In reality, gender issues connected to domestic violence are more complicated.

Findings on whether women are at greater risk of intimate partner violence than men vary from survey to survey. On its website, the National Institute of Justice (NIJ) states that the National Violence Against Women Survey conducted by the NIJ and the federal Centers for Disease Control and Prevention found that women experience significantly more intimate partner violence than do men, whereas the National Family Violence Survey concluded that men and women are equally likely to be physically assaulted by an intimate partner. In a 2007 article in the *American Journal of Public Health*, researchers cited nearly 250 scholarly studies demonstrating that women were at least as likely as men to engage in intimate partner violence. Furthermore, a study of the causes of domestic violence reported by John Hamel and Tonia Nicholls in *Family Interventions in Domestic Violence* (2007) found that twelve of the fourteen reasons cited for aggression applied equally to men and women, with self-defense being a minor motive for both sexes. Some findings, however, are generally consistent from survey to survey. Women are more likely than men to be injured by domestic violence, as men tend to use more violent forms of aggression. Additionally, both sexes are equally capable of emotional abuse.

The incidence of intimate partner violence against women varies significantly from country to country. According to the World Health Organization's *World Report on Violence and Health*, the percentage of women assaulted by an intimate partner in a twelve-month period ranged from 3 percent or less in the United States, Canada, and Australia to 27 percent in Leon, Nicaragua, whereas 38 percent of married women in the Republic of Korea and 52 percent of married Palestinian women in the West Bank and Gaza Strip are assaulted by intimate partners. The report cites research that suggests cultural reasons for these differences:

> In more traditional societies, wife beating is largely regarded as a consequence of a man's right to inflict physical punishment on his wife—something indicated by studies from countries as diverse as Bangladesh, Cambodia, India, Mexico, Nigeria, Pakistan, Papua New Guinea, the United Republic of Tanzania, and Zimbabwe. Cultural justifications for violence usually follow from traditional notions of the proper roles of men and women.

Exposure to violence as a child affects boys and girls differently. For both sexes, exposure to violence tends to desensitize children to violence, making them more likely to engage in or tolerate violent behavior as adults. Boys exposed to domestic violence in childhood are more likely than other males to use violence in intimate partner relationships in adulthood, whereas girls exposed to domestic violence in childhood are more apt to tolerate violence from their intimate partners in adulthood, according to numerous experts, including Canadian social worker Gary Direnfeld.

The viewpoints in this chapter explore the differences and similarities in male and female domestic violence, focusing on the many complexities of the issue.

Understanding Intimate Partner Violence

Centers for Disease Control and Prevention

The Centers for Disease Control and Prevention (CDC) is a federal public health agency within the US Department of Health and Human Services.

Intimate partner violence (IPV) occurs between two people in a close relationship. The term "intimate partner" includes current and former spouses and dating partners. IPV exists along a continuum from a single episode of violence to ongoing battering.

IPV includes four types of behavior:

Physical violence is when a person hurts or tries to hurt a partner by hitting, kicking, or other type of physical force.

Sexual violence is forcing a partner to take part in a sex act when the partner does not consent.

Threats of physical or sexual violence include the use of words, gestures, weapons, or other means to communicate the intent to cause harm.

Emotional abuse is threatening a partner or his or her possessions or loved ones, or harming a partner's sense of self-worth. Examples are stalking, name-calling, intimidation, or not letting a partner see friends and family.

Often, IPV starts with emotional abuse. This behavior can progress to physical or sexual assault. Several types of IPV may occur together.

Centers for Disease Control and Prevention, "Understanding Intimate Partner Violence," 2012.

IPV is a serious problem in the United States:

Nearly 3 in 10 women and 1 in 10 men in the US have experienced rape, physical violence, and/or stalking by a partner with IPV-related impact.

IPV resulted in 2,340 deaths in 2007. Of these deaths, 70% were females and 30% were males.

The medical care, mental health services, and lost productivity (e.g., time away from work) cost of IPV was an estimated $5.8 billion in 1995. Updated to 2003 dollars, that's more than $8.3 billion.

Victims often have low self-esteem. They may have a hard time trusting others and being in relationships.

These numbers underestimate the problem. Many victims do not report IPV to police, friends, or family. Victims may think others will not believe them or that the police cannot help.

How Does IPV Affect Health?

IPV can affect health in many ways. The longer the violence goes on, the more serious the effects.

Many victims suffer physical injuries. Some are minor, like cuts, scratches, bruises, and welts. Others are more serious and can cause death or disabilities. These include broken bones, internal bleeding, and head trauma.

Not all injuries are physical. IPV can also cause emotional harm. Victims may have trauma symptoms. This includes flashbacks, panic attacks, and trouble sleeping. Victims often have low self-esteem. They may have a hard time trusting others and being in relationships. The anger and stress that victims feel may lead to eating disorders and depression. Some victims even think about or commit suicide.

IPV is linked to harmful health behaviors as well. Victims may try to cope with their trauma in unhealthy ways. This includes smoking, drinking, taking drugs, or having risky sex.

Who Is at Risk for IPV?

Several factors can increase the risk that someone will hurt his or her partner. However, having these risk factors does not always mean that IPV will occur. Risk factors for perpetration (hurting a partner) include:

Being violent or aggressive in the past

Seeing or being a victim of violence as a child

Using drugs or alcohol, especially drinking heavily

Not having a job or other life events that cause stress

How Can We Prevent IPV?

The goal is to stop IPV before it begins. There is a lot to learn about how to prevent IPV. We do know that strategies that promote healthy behaviors in relationships are important. Programs that teach young people skills for dating can prevent violence. These programs can stop violence in dating relationships before it occurs.

We know less about how to prevent IPV in adults. However, some programs that teach healthy relationship skills seem to help stop violence before it ever starts.

Men and Women Have Different Patterns of Intimate Partner Violence

Marianne Hester

Marianne Hester is a professor at the School for Policy Studies at the University of Bristol in the United Kingdom.

National representative surveys indicate that while men and women in heterosexual relationships may experience similar domestic violence behaviours, there are also important differences. For instance, women experience a greater amount and more severe abuse from male partners. The recent [2008] British Crime Survey data on partner abuse found that a fifth of men, 22%, and a third of women, 33%, had experienced abuse from a partner since the age of 16, and that the physical and emotional impacts on female victims were significantly greater than on male victims. Echoing this gender distinction regarding the impacts of domestic violence and abuse, men tended not to report partner abuse to the police because they considered the incident *"too trivial or not worth reporting."*

Data on the prevalence of heterosexual domestic abuse in general populations thus show larger differences between men's and women's experiences of domestic violence when impact is also taken into account. As a consequence, women are the largest group to seek help and be in contact with services. Based on research with female victims, we may also expect that domestic violence reported to the police involves behaviours (whether physical, sexual, psychological, emotional, verbal, financial etc.) used as an ongoing pattern of fear and

Marianne Hester, "Who Does What to Whom? Gender and Domestic Violence Perpetrators," *Violence Against Women Research Group School for Policy Studies*, University of Bristol in association with the Northern Rock Foundation, June 2009, pp. 1–19. All rights reserved. Reproduced by permission.

coercive control by one person against another with whom they have or have had a relationship. Such 'archetypal' domestic violence (or 'intimate terrorism') will usually involve one partner being violent, involve frequent abuse, and is likely to escalate and to result in serious injury. Within this context it has been found that women, in particular, may use 'violent resistance' against violent male partners. Echoing this, women's use of violence has been found in a number of studies to be defensive or retaliatory rather than initiating.

Alcohol use of one or both partners can . . . impact on the boundaries between victim and perpetrator.

In the US a pro-arrest policy was implemented from the early 1990s, and has been taken further than in the UK, with mandatory arrest and prosecution in some US locations. The approach has resulted in a notable increase in the number of women being arrested for perpetrating domestic violence in the US. [W.] DeLeon-Granados [and colleagues] suggest that this increase may be the result of the police becoming more 'real' about violence where they previously minimised that by women. Also, that male perpetrators may be manipulating the system resulting in disproportionate arrests of women. [S.L.] Miller, for instance, found that the men may ring the police first in order to pre-empt women asking for help.

In addition, a systematic review of the literature has found that men may be over-reporting instances of being victims of domestic violence while at the same time being perpetrators of domestic violence. The alcohol use of one or both partners can also impact on the boundaries between victim and perpetrator with subsequent difficulties in assessing risk and in determination of who is the primary aggressor.

These issues have led to further questions in the current rescarch about:

- The extent and severity of the domestic violence and gender of the perpetrator.

- How 'sole perpetrator' violence might differ depending on whether it is a male or a female perpetrator.

- Men's and women's use of domestic violence where both partners are making allegations.

- Whether there has been an increase over time in women recorded or arrested as domestic violence perpetrators.

Current Research Method

The current research uses and builds on the data from two previous research projects also funded by the Northern Rock Foundation: the research on attrition and domestic violence cases going through the criminal justice system; and the research on domestic violence perpetrator profiles, identification of their needs and early intervention.

In April 2001, Northumbria Police introduced a computer-based system for recording and linking domestic violence incidents across all police districts. Using this database the previous attrition study developed an initial picture of incidents, attrition and police practice across three police districts and in relation to three time periods—April 2001, June 2001 and March 2002. The second study developed 692 perpetrator longitudinal profiles, and analysed the 1,889 incidents related to these individuals. The 692 profiles involved tracking the 356 perpetrators from the attrition study to provide a 3-year picture, combined with a further 336 domestic perpetrators sampled from the first week of November 2004 and tracked until the end of July 2005.

In the current research, three separate, longitudinal, and comparative samples, 96 cases overall, were developed from the previous 692 perpetrator profiles. This included a total of 126 individuals identified as perpetrators. . . .

Comparison of the 96 cases where men, women or both were recorded by the police as domestic violence perpetrators, revealed a number of clear differences between these groups as well as other important patterns. Analysis of the police and interview data indicated differences by gender, including the nature of incidents, levels of repeat perpetration, arrest and conviction. There were also some differences between cases involving sole perpetrators and where both men and women were recorded as dual perpetrators. Further issues included use of alcohol and drugs, illness, children and age.

The difference between men and women was stark, with men significantly more likely to be repeat perpetrators.

When Do Incidents Take Place?

The largest proportion of cases related to couples still together in a relationship (nearly half the cases—48%). Just over a quarter involved violence post-separation of the partners (27%). The remaining cases involved couples in process of separation with incidents recorded both during the relationship and also after separation (25%).

Gender and Incidents

Generally individuals were recorded as having been perpetrators in between one and 52 incidents of domestic violence. However, the difference between men and women was stark, with men significantly more likely to be repeat perpetrators. The vast majority of men had at least two incidents recorded (83%), many a lot more than that, and one man had 52 incidents recorded within the six year tracking period. In contrast, nearly two-thirds of women recorded as perpetrators had only one incident recorded (62%), and the highest number of repeat incidents for any woman was eight. These data indicate that the intensity and severity of violence and abusive behaviours from the men was much more extreme. This is also reflected in the nature of the violence used.

According to the incidents described by the police, men were significantly more likely than women to use physical violence, threats, and harassment. While verbal abuse was used in most incidents by both men and women, men were also slightly more likely to be verbally abusive. Men were more likely to damage the women's property, while the women were more likely to damage their own. Men's violence tended to create a context of fear and related to that, control. This was not similarly the case where women were perpetrators.

Incidents with women as perpetrators mainly involved verbal abuse, some physical violence, and only small proportions involved threat or harassment. However, women were much more likely to use a weapon, although this was at times in order to stop further violence from their partners. The police descriptions also characterised female perpetrators as to a greater extent having mental health or other health issues. The police were more likely to question whether they had identified the correct perpetrator in instances involving women.

Violence used by men against female partners was much more severe than that used by women against men.

More Men Arrested Overall

As might be expected from the nature and severity of the domestic violence incidents, there were more arrests overall of men than of women. All cases with seven or more incidents, most of which involved men, led to arrest at some time. This echoes US findings that male domestic violence perpetrators have more extensive criminal histories than female perpetrators. None the less, women were arrested to a disproportionate degree given the fewer incidents where they were perpetrators. Women were three times more likely to be arrested. During the six year tracking period 47 (73% of all male perpetrators) and 36 women (56% of all female perpetrators) were arrested, with men arrested once in every ten incidents (in 11% of incidents) and women arrested every three incidents (in 32% of incidents)....

Breach of the Peace was the highest level of offence for which most men and women were arrested. Men were most likely to have actual bodily harm, criminal damage or other offences (including affray [fighting in public] and drunk and disorderly) as the highest levels of offences resulting in arrest. Men were arrested for threats to kill, but not women. In contrast (and reflecting women's use of weapons), violence by women resulted in arrests for a wider range of, and more serious, offences involving assault—from common assault, to grievous bodily harm to grievous bodily harm with intent.

Men appeared more likely than women to be charged or cautioned. This was the case for a quarter of the men (16/63, 25%) and only one in six [sic] of the women (5/62, 8%). According to the data available, the charges resulted in three of the men being convicted (for Breach of the Peace, assault and criminal damage), and one of the women being convicted (for Breach of the Peace)....

Important Conclusions

The research found that:

1. While cases were very varied, there were distinct patterns by gender, with significant differences between male and female perpetrators of domestic violence in many respects.

2. A vastly greater number of incidents were attributed to men, as either sole or dual perpetrators.

3. Violence used by men against female partners was much more severe than that used by women against men, and a greater proportion of male perpetrators were also arrested.

4. The number of women recorded or arrested as domestic violence perpetrators had increased slightly over time.

5. Men and women appeared to experience and use violent/abusive behaviour in different ways, with violence by men more likely to involve fear by and control of victims.

6. Cases where men and women were both recorded as perpetrators were more varied than those involving sole perpetrators, and included the largest number of repeat incidents.

7. The majority of the perpetrators appeared to abuse alcohol to some degree, especially men, and more often in cases involving dual perpetrators. Abuse of alcohol was also more likely to lead to arrest.

8. The police generally identified just one perpetrator and one victim in relation to each incident.

9. Children were present in the majority of incidents, and some incidents were related to child contact.

10. Women were more likely to use weapons, and often in order to protect themselves.

11. Men and women who were victims appeared to refuse to give statements, or to withdraw statements, for different reasons.

Men and Women Have Different Responses to Childhood Abuse

Ad Hoc Working Group on Women, Mental Health, Mental Illness, and Addictions

The Ad Hoc Working Group on Women, Mental Health, Mental Illness, and Addictions is a group of researchers and community workers formed by the Canadian Women's Health Network in 2006.

Violence and trauma, including childhood abuse, sexual abuse, and intimate partner violence, are common in Canada. It is conservatively estimated that half of all Canadian women and one-third of Canadian men have survived at least one incidence of sexual or physical violence. Although both boys and girls are affected by family violence, four out of five victims of family-related sexual assaults (79%) are girls.

Heather Pollett writes in *The Connection Between Violence, Trauma and Mental Illness in Women* that the relationship between trauma and mental health is a complex one; not all people who experience abuse, either in childhood or adulthood, inevitably develop a mental illness, and not everyone who has been diagnosed with a mental illness has experienced abuse. Yet research has established a strong association between trauma, violence and mental health. Those reporting a history of childhood physical abuse have significantly higher rates of anxiety disorders, alcohol dependence and antisocial behaviour, and are more likely to have one or more disorders than were those without such a history.

Ad Hoc Working Group on Women, Mental Health, Mental Illness and Addictions, "Making the Links: Violence, Trauma and Mental Health," *Network*, v. 11, no. 2, Spring/Summer 2009, p. 6. All rights reserved. Reproduced by permission.

Research by H. MacMillan et al. found that women with a history of physical abuse have "significantly higher lifetime rates of major depression and illicit drug abuse/dependence than did women with no history." This association was not found in men. For men the prevalence of disorders tended to be higher among those who report exposure to sexual abuse, but only with associations to alcohol dependence. Therefore, the relationship between a childhood history of physical abuse and lifetime psychopathology (mental illness or disorder) varies significantly by gender. A similar relationship has been seen between a childhood history of sexual abuse and lifetime psychopathology.

Epidemiological studies have also shown that the risk of developing Post Traumatic Stress Disorder (PTSD) among those exposed to violence is approximately twofold higher in women and that women often experience a characteristic cluster of symptoms that has been named "complex PTSD." Vulnerability factors may include: women's greater likelihood of exposure to assaultive violence, societal influences, gendered meanings ascribed to traumatic experiences, and hormonal influences.

Reasons for Disclosure

The reasons men and women do not disclose personal trauma such as experiences of childhood sexual violence may differ as well; studies have shown that males report difficulty disclosing because they fear being viewed as homosexual and as victims, while women's difficulties centre on feeling conflicted about responsibility, and they more strongly anticipate being blamed or not believed.

For women, problems most commonly associated with the experience of violence include: depression, anxiety, posttraumatic stress disorder, personality disorders, dissociative identity disorder, psychosis, and eating disorders. For men, childhood maltreatment has been associated with problem alcohol use. Women make three to four times more suicide attempts than men (though men succeed more often than women). The Ontario Canadian Mental Health Association has found that there is a significant correlation between a history of sexual abuse and the lifetime number of suicide attempts, and this correlation is twice as strong for women as for men.

Misdiagnosis and inappropriate mental health treatment can also reinforce self-destructive behaviours.

Pollett writes that individuals who have experienced violence, like others dealing with mental health problems, face mental health treatments that are primarily based on the biomedical model (focused on biological and genetic factors of mental health instead of social determinants such as poverty, housing, stigma and past experiences of violence). Women who require mental health services often receive inappropriate diagnoses and treatment or are denied services because their behaviour is misunderstood or stigmatized.

She also writes that borderline personality disorder (BPD), for example, is diagnosed in women at three times the rate of men. Women with this diagnosis may be more often in crisis situations and access health resources more frequently than men because BPD is considered difficult to treat. It has been shown that if the symptoms of BPD are not recognized as trauma-related and treated as such, these women may be at increased risk for violence or even suicide. Misdiagnosis and inappropriate mental health treatment can also reinforce self-destructive behaviours such as drug and alcohol use.

Men and women who do not receive appropriate care for trauma, mental health and addictions problems may end up falling through the cracks and end up within the correctional system. A study found that the pathways between childhood abuse and neglect and violent criminal behaviour are different for men and women; for men childhood maltreatment has both a direct effect on aggressive behaviour and an indirect one, through alcohol, while for women, only the indirect path was found.

In Canada, 82% of federally sentenced women have reported past sexual and/or physical abuse, and the rate increases to 90% for Aboriginal women. The Elizabeth Fry Society reports that more federally sentenced women than men have received a diagnosis of mental illness and their issues tend to be different. For instance, women in federal correctional institutions have a higher rate of self-mutilation and attempted suicide than their male counterparts.

Substance Use

Substance use and mental health problems frequently co-occur among people who are survivors of violence, trauma and abuse, often in complex, indirect, mutually reinforcing ways. Many women identify substance use as a way to cope with gender-based abuse and trauma. Nancy Poole writes in *Gender Does Matter: Coalescing on Women and Substance Use* that alcohol problems have been found to be up to 15 times higher among women survivors of partner violence than in the general population. Yet service providers and policy-makers have not always acted on these connections; services with a primary mandate for domestic violence and sexual assault have often not served women with substance use problems, adding to women's vulnerability. Addiction services also must integrate work on trauma, provide information on the connections with addiction recovery and offer individual and group programming.

Effective Models of Care

The lack of gender-specific responses to the linked issues of violence, trauma, substance use, and mental health problems has resulted in significant costs for service systems: women and men with trauma histories are likely to repeatedly use emergency rooms, mental health inpatient units, and/or end up in the criminal justice system as they cope with symptoms in a context of unresponsive health and social policies and programs. A study found that women who reported a history of childhood sexual trauma were more likely to visit emergency rooms and had annual total health care costs which were significantly higher than women without such a history (these costs were still observed after excluding the costs of mental health care). It has also been shown that adult women victims of sexual trauma use higher levels of health care (more physician visits and higher outpatient costs) when compared to women who have experienced other forms of violence.

The application of a gender-based analysis has assisted health systems and communities in developing evidence-based models that provide effective, integrated, gender-specific care to women and men for violence, trauma, substance use, and mental health issues. For example, the Women, Co-occurring Disorders and Violence Study (funded by the US Substance Abuse and Mental Health Services Administration) found that women-centred, integrated services that provide linked supports for women with trauma, substance use, and mental health problems were more effective in facilitating recovery than usual care, and cost no more to provide. Similarly, the Warriors Against Violence Society in Vancouver has used gender-specific and culturally relevant programming to effectively and compassionately assist Aboriginal men, youth, and families to identify and respond to the root causes of violence against women and children in Aboriginal communities.

Gender-Based Violence Is a Special Problem for African American Women

Tricia B. Bent-Goodley

Tricia B. Bent-Goodley is a professor at the Howard University School of Social Work in Washington, DC.

It is estimated that one out of three women and girls across the world experience GBV [gender-based violence]. In a World Health Organization study on women's health and domestic violence within 10 countries, physical violence, sexual violence, or both existed among 15 percent to 71 percent of the women. In another multicountry study on domestic violence, between 21 percent and 58 percent of the women surveyed experienced physical and sexual violence in their lifetime, and between 17 percent and 48 percent of these women experienced the same type of violence at the hands of an intimate partner. Intimate partner violence (IPV) is the most common of these types of violence. In a review of 70 population-based studies, the rate of IPV among women was between 10 percent and 60 percent. In country after country, the statistics are staggering: Nearly 50 percent of women in Bangladesh have experienced IPV from a male partner; 80 percent of women in Pakistan have experienced IPV from a male partner; and every 83 seconds, a woman is raped in South Africa, with only 20 percent of these women reporting the case to police annually.

The United States is not exempt from these forms of violence. More than 30 percent of U.S. women have reported experiencing physical or sexual abuse by a husband or boyfriend each year, with estimates as high as 5 million U.S. women experiencing domestic violence each year. African American women have been particularly vulnerable to more lethal forms of violence and greater severity of violence than other groups of women. Women of color face increased barriers to treatment and are less likely to obtain services that are culturally responsive and, hence, more targeted at the social and cultural contexts in which they live. African American women are also more likely to have their children removed from the home and become incarcerated under mandatory arrest laws compared with women from other ethnic groups. African American women are more likely to be resistant to receiving services for fear of being treated poorly or misunderstood by the practitioner. They have also experienced discriminatory treatment; for example, African American women have been turned away from services, arrested, and prosecuted because of negative stereotypes.

A Public Health Issue

Increasingly, GBV has been acknowledged as a serious reproductive, sexual, psychosocial, and public health issue for women. Women who have experienced GBV have been more likely to experience poorer health, chronic pain, memory loss, spontaneous and induced abortion, and greater abuse during pregnancy. The connection between GBV and HIV has also received increasing attention as the rates of HIV are soaring in communities of African ancestry around the world. GBV diminishes a woman's ability to negotiate condom usage, can interfere with her ability to obtain needed medical or drug treatment, and can place her at risk of violence if it is determined that she has HIV/AIDS. Having a history of forced sex places women and girls at an even greater risk of contracting HIV/ AIDS. Finding solutions to this problem must include a culturally based approach.

Cultural Responses to Gender-Based Violence

Because GBV touches the lives of people from such diverse cultures, it requires a culturally based approach. The different social and cultural contexts are critical to developing responses that are effective and make sense to the particular population. Women of color have acknowledged the importance of looking not only at race, ethnicity, and class, but also at how they intersect to make women even more vulnerable to violence and other forms of oppression. As such, stereotypes of women of color, lack of trust of outsiders and public officials, and fear of reporting due to the potential for discriminatory treatment and further violence are all reasons that women of color have given for why services should be culturally grounded and based on the recommendations of women in the community. Interventions should be holistic and should not just focus on the individual; they should include an emphasis on the pervasive social ills, formidable health challenges, social and economic inequities, community perceptions, and social hierarchies that perpetuate these issues. . . .

> *Black people in traditional Africa, slavery, and rural life after emancipation . . . had their own ways of identifying problems and their own tools of intervention.*

There are strengths among African Americans that can be used to respond to domestic violence. The BEBSW [Black Experience-Based Social Work] approach builds on these strengths. BEBSW stands out as one way of addressing this complex issue through a culturally based approach. Using this approach does not dishonor the great variation and diversity of historical and contemporary experiences within the African American community, but, instead, builds on the notion of connectedness that still exists within this rich culture. BEBSW "draw[s] from a social work emphasis on black experiences, black values, black perspectives, and black methods of problem solving" and asserts "that black people in traditional Africa, slavery, and rural life after emancipation . . . had their own ways of identifying problems and their own tools of intervention" [according to E.P. Martin and J.M. Martin].

African Americans have developed effective mechanisms to address social and community problems. BEBSW allows providers to build on that tradition. Martin and Martin argued that at the heart of many social problems in the black community is the struggle to deal with being separated from and losing family and friends. As a result, the three major concepts of BEBSW are moaning, mourning, and morning: "a linear progression from suffering (moaning) to collective healing and support (mourning) and finally toward an ideal state of health, happiness, and transformation (morning)." Each concept is centered on the problem of separation and loss and the associated historical and contemporary trauma. . . .

BEBSW provides a means or examining GBV from a culturally specific perspective and offers ways of responding to GBV. Using a black perspective, BEBSW roots the assessment, interventions, and healing from within a culturally responsive framework that posits change on multiple levels, including the individual, family, community, and societal levels. The BEBSW approach offers a framework to better understand how GBV is unique within the black experience. The approach reinforces the importance of instilling hope and addressing issues of separation and loss, both through death and non-death. Included in BEBSW is the need to focus on culturally specific grief and community education approaches that evidence respect and awareness of the diversity, strengths, and challenges within this population. Social workers are uniquely and irreplaceably prepared to address the problem of GBV by offering new culturally specific strategies, enhanced advocacy, and greater awareness of this issue.

Family Violence Is a Human Problem, Not a Gender Problem

John Hamel

John Hamel is a social worker whose clinical services include family violence assessments and treatment programs for abusive men, women, and families. He is the author of Gender-Inclusive Treatment of Intimate Partner Abuse: A Comprehensive Approach.

The causes of intimate partner abuse are far more similar between the genders than they are dissimilar. There is evidence that male gender role stress and gender-role conflict are correlated with male-perpetrated partner abuse. Patriarchal beliefs may also be a contributing factor in some male-perpetrated partner abuse, but are less important than harboring pro-violent attitudes, which is a risk factor for both genders. In their review of the risk factor literature, [R.] Medeiros and [M.] Straus found no significant gender differences in the relationship between partner violence and 72–73 percent of the major IPV [intimate partner violence] risk factors. The same direction of effect was found in 99 percent of the total number. Risk factors found in male populations that have also been found among females include (1) growing up in a violent home, (2) certain personality traits such as dependency and jealousy, which are common among both heterosexual and lesbian offenders, (3) and conditions that either meet the criterion for a DSM [*Diagnostic and Statistical Manual of Mental Disorders*] Axis II personality disorder (borderline, an-

John Hamel, "Toward a Gender-Inclusive Conception of Intimate Partner Violence Research and Theory: Part 2—New Directions," *International Journal of Men's Health*, v. 8, no. 1, Spring 2009, p. 41. All rights reserved. Reproduced by permission. Men's Studies Press, LLC. Copyright 2012.

tisocial, or narcissistic) or are characterized by a generally aggressive personality. In the study by [K.] Henning et al., which compared men and women participants in batterer intervention programs, the women scored higher on the Millon Clinical Multiaxial Inventory III for 8 of the 14 maladaptive personality subscales measured, including compulsive, histrionic, narcissistic, paranoid, borderline and sadistic traits. Whether these elevated traits mean that partner assaultive women are more pathological than partner assaultive men in general, or that it takes a pathological woman to come to the attention of a law enforcement system predisposed to arrest males, was not determined by the study.

Intimate partner abuse is a complex phenomenon.

Similar correlations have been found for men and women between perpetration of IPV and proximal risk factors such as unemployment and low socioeconomic status, being under 30 years of age, or being in a dating or cohabitating relationship. The review by Medeiros and Straus also identified relationship conflict as a significant risk factor for both genders. Partly due to ... negative communication dynamics ..., conflicted couples are at risk for physical violence. Once there is abuse by either partner, there is a greater risk of continued reciprocal abuse. [J.] Stets found a high correlation for both genders between psychological abuse victimization and perpetration. The greatest risk factor for physical violence perpetration in the [J.] White, [L.] Merrill and [M.] Kos study of 2,784 Navy recruits was physical or psychological victimization by one's partner. A [2005] study by [N.] Graham-Kevan and [J.] Archer of 358 female students and staff at an English university found no correlation between fear and a woman's use of severe violence. Significant effects, however, were found for reciprocal violence as a means of retribution or as the result of a desire to control one's partner.

These studies suggest that intimate partner abuse is a complex phenomenon, driven by factors inherent in the individual (including culturally-derived attitudes and beliefs), situational variables, and the particular dynamics of the relationship. Recent studies on adult attachment are especially promising. As was the case with personality characteristics, research on attachment focused first on men, and only later expanded to a consideration of the attachment styles of both partners and the interplay between them. Now we know that relationships in which one partner fears intimacy (avoidant or fearful attachment) and the other fears abandonment (preoccupied or fearful attachment) are at higher risk for physical abuse, and that violence may be initiated by individuals with different attachment styles, and by either gender. . . .

Disproportional Treatment

There is no doubt that women are physically affected more by IPV than are men, suffering a greater share of injuries, especially those that are life-threatening. Because of this and women's greater fear of physical harm, it cannot be said that "domestic violence is the same" between the genders. However, in light of similar etiology, the comparable rates of both physical and psychological abuse and coercive tactics, and how they affect men and women, the consequences of mother-perpetrated IPV on children, the family system, and the intergenerational transmission of violence, women's higher rates of injuries ought not be cited as an excuse to maintain the status quo. Women suffer greater physical injury not because men are meaner or more privileged, pathological or controlling, and [according to researcher B. Morse] "not necessarily because men strike more often, but because men strike harder." That men strike harder means that safety planning should be a relatively greater concern for female victims and that women will require the greater share of shelter beds. It does not, however, justify the disproportionately high rates of arrest and mandatory treatment for men relative to women, or the scant availability of services for male victims. Surely, we can do better.

Women Are as Likely as Men to Abuse a Partner

Murray A. Straus

Murray A. Straus is a professor of sociology and the founder and codirector of the Family Research Laboratory at the University of New Hampshire.

Despite a large body of high-quality evidence, gender symmetry in the perpetration of physical assault against a partner in a marital, cohabiting, or dating relationship has not been perceived by the public or service providers. Moreover, . . . research showing symmetry has often been concealed and denied by academics. The term "gender symmetry" will be used to refer to approximately equal rates of perpetration of physical assault by women and men, and similar patterns of motivation and risk factors. . . .

Because concealment and denial of PV [partner violence] by women has been so effective, many readers will not be familiar with the evidence on gender symmetry. . . . The percentage of women who physically assaulted a male partner is as high or higher than the percentage of men who physically assaulted a female partner, and that this applies to severe violence such as kicking, choking, and attacks with objects and weapons, as well as to minor violence. . . . Women *initiate* PV at the same or higher rates as men, and they are the sole perpetrator at the same or higher rates. Moreover . . . the evidence demonstrating similar rates of PV perpetration have been available for at least 25 years. . . .

There is one important and consistently reported gender difference in PV: although women engage in both minor and

Murray A. Straus, "Why the Overwhelming Evidence on Partner Physical Violence by Women Has Not Been Perceived and Is Often Denied," *Journal of Aggression, Maltreatment & Trauma*, v. 18, 2009, pp. 552–71. All rights reserved. Reproduced by permission of Taylor & Francis Group, LLC., http://www.taylorandfrancis.com

severe violence as often as men, the adverse effects on victims are much greater for women. Attacks by men cause more injury (both physical and psychological), more deaths, and more fear. In addition, women are more often economically trapped in a violent relationship than men because women continue to earn less than men, and because when a marriage ends, women have custodial responsibility for children at least 80% of the time. The greater adverse effect on women is an extremely important difference, and it indicates the need to continue to provide more services for female victims of PV than for male victims. In addition, ... the greater adverse effect on women underlies the reluctance to acknowledge the evidence on gender symmetry. However, empathy for women because of the greater injury and the need to help victimized women must not be allowed to obscure the fact that men sustain about a third of the injuries from PV, including a third of the deaths by homicide. PV by women is therefore a serious crime, health, and social problem that must be addressed, even though the effects are not as prevalent as assaults perpetrated by male partners. Moreover, the risk of injury and the probability of the violence continuing or escalating is greatest when both partners are violent, as is the case for at least half of violent couples. . . .

Evidence Is Concealed from the Public

A major factor in understanding why the public does not perceive the extent of female PV is that the information has not been made available or has been distorted in the media, which are the public's main sources of information. Media coverage of PV reflects and reinforces ... gender stereotypes. . . . For example, a study of newspaper coverage of the 785 homicides that occurred in Cincinnati, Ohio over a 17-year period found that 79% of partner homicides perpetrated by men were reported, compared to 50% of the partner homicides perpetrated by women. Moreover, for cases of women killed by a male partner there was a mean of 3.5 articles, compared to a mean of 1.7 articles for men killed by a female partner.

Another example (from, literally, thousands) is "And Then He Hit Me" in the *American Association of Retired People Magazine*, which states that the number of woman-on-man incidents of domestic violence among the elderly is "negligible" and cites as the source a study by [K.] Pillemer and [D.] Finkelhor. But that study found that 43% of the cases of physical violence of the elderly were the wife assaulting the husband, whereas only 17% were husbands assaulting their wife. This probably reflects the fact that many more wives than husbands have the responsibility of providing care for elderly, infirm, and often difficult-to-deal-with partners. . . .

Women's advocates most often focus on the relatively small proportion of overall PV that is visible to justice, shelter, batterer intervention, and other service providers.

In addition to failing to perceive the extent of gender symmetry in PV, there have also been strenuous efforts by researchers and other academics to deny the overwhelming evidence, including punishment of researchers who have persisted in publishing results showing gender symmetry, such as denial of tenure. . . .

Academics Have Concealed Evidence

One of the most important reasons for denial of gender symmetry is failure to adequately recognize heterogeneity [differences] in PV. Women's advocates most often focus on the relatively small proportion of overall PV that is visible to justice, shelter, batterer intervention, and other service providers (i.e., cases in which women's injury, fear, and domination are much more common). In contrast, the research showing gender symmetry has been based on general population samples in which the predominant form of PV is minor, bidirectional, not physically injurious, and often not fear provoking for men, even when it should be. The findings of these general population studies are not believed by battered women's advocates because they are inconsistent with the characteristic of the actual cases they work with every day.

Academics are the ones who know or produce the research and are the ones who have concealed, denied, or hidden the evidence. One example is the belief that when women are violent, it is almost always an act of self-defense, whereas the previously cited studies (and others not cited) show that this is rarely the case. Instead of concealing and denying, academic advisors of service providers should help them understand the heterogeneity of severity and motives that characterize PV. This can help provide more effective prevention and treatment programs that take heterogeneity into account....

A Perceived Threat to Feminism

The women's movement brought public attention to the fact that PV may be the most prevalent form of interpersonal violence and to the plight of women victims. The feminist effort created a world-wide determination to cease ignoring PV, and to take steps to combat PV. Feminists have largely been responsible for changing police and court practices from ignoring and minimizing PV to compelling the criminal justice system to attend and intervene. That change in police practices is only one of the many ways in which the women's movement has changed social norms tolerating male-to-female PV. In addition, feminists have created two important new social institutions: shelters for battered women and treatment programs for male perpetrators. Because the well-being of women is the primary concern of the feminist effort, their approach appropriately focused on protecting women from male violence.

The problem with this approach is not just the almost exclusive focus on female victims and male perpetrators. The problem is also insistence on a single-cause theory: the belief that PV is a reflection of a patriarchal social and family system. Subsequent research has shown that there are many causes of PV and great variability in types of violent relationships.

The removal of patriarchy as the main cause of PV weakens a dramatic example of the harmful effects of patriarchy.

This research has also shown that women perpetrate PV as much as or more than men, and that although some PV is "gendered" in the sense of an effort by men as a category to dominate women as a category, most is traceable to a number of other risk factors. For frequent severe PV, psychopathology such as antisocial personality and borderline personality is frequent; and for "ordinary" or "situational" violence, poor anger management, and frustration and anger at misbehavior by the partner are frequent precipitants of PV. The evidence on these risk factors and motives is difficult to square with the patriarchal theory of PV because the two central tenants of the patriarchal theory are male perpetration, motivated by efforts to maintain a male-dominant family and social system. I suggest that one of reasons for the denial is to maintain adherence to the patriarchal theory of PV.

In addition to being perceived as a threat to the theory that had inspired and sustained the battered women's movement, I suggest that the research showing gender symmetry has been denied because it may have been perceived as a threat to feminism in general. This is because a key step in the effort to achieve an equalitarian society is to bring about recognition of the harm that a patriarchal system causes. The removal of patriarchy as the main cause of PV weakens a dramatic example of the harmful effects of patriarchy. That is unfortunate, but by no means critical because the effort to achieve equality can continue to be made on the basis of many other ways in which women continue to be subordinate to men (e.g., efforts to rectify the differential). . . .

There is a fear that if the public, legislators, and administrators believed the research on gender symmetry, it would weaken support for services to female victims, such as shelters for battered women, and weaken efforts to arrest and prosecute violent men. I know of no cases in which funding for services for female victims has been decreased because "women are also violent." Nevertheless, I have been told on several occasions that I am endangering services for battered women by publishing the results of research showing equal perpetration. . . .

Fear of Undermining Efforts

There is also a fear that efforts to arrest and prosecute male offenders will be undermined by acknowledging female PV, and that women will be unjustly prosecuted for violence perpetrated in self-defense. In fact, a growing number of women are being arrested through the introduction of mandatory or recommended arrest for PV. For example, in California between 1987 and 1997, the ratio of male and female arrests for PV decreased from 1 female arrest to 18 male arrests to a ratio of 1 to 4.5. It is unlikely that this shift is a result of an increase in female violence. Rates of both fatal and nonfatal PV have been dropping over time and such marked shifts in female perpetration are not found for other crimes. I suggest that fear of weakening arrest of men and, more recently, increasing arrest of women is part of the reason for concealing the evidence. However, in my opinion, the main factor contributing to increased arrest of women is the success of the effort by the women's movement to change police practice from one of avoiding interference in "domestic disturbances" to one of mandatory or recommended arrest.

Another concern that may have motivated the concealment and denial is the fear that recognizing the complexity of

PV, including acknowledging female PV, will weaken the ability of the justice system to act on behalf of women victims of PV. The prototypical cases that galvanized efforts to ensure that women received swift police response, followed by arrest and prosecution of their partners, were of nonviolent women who are terrorized by their partners and needed the assistance of the legal system to escape. I suggest that those concerned with protecting female victims fear that if this image of PV is lost—and instead the justice system has to assess the context of the incident, the history of both partners, the motive for the offense, and the level of fear generated—the difficulty and burden of doing that may result in failing to adequately protect women and prosecute male offenders. . . .

Consequences of the Denial

In denying the evidence, social scientists are also doing a disservice to women. They are hindering efforts to help women avoid engaging in PV. This is important because women, like men, need to be helped to recognize that hitting a partner is morally wrong, criminal, and harmful to the perpetrator as well as to the victim. First, it is associated with lower levels of relationship health. Second, it increases the probability of physical attacks by the woman's partner. Third, it exposes children to the well-documented harm from witnessing PV, and those consequences also apply when the perpetrator is the mother.

Finally, just as denial of painful phenomena by individuals is usually harmful, denial by social groups is likely to be harmful to the group engaged in the denial. I am concerned that denial of the evidence on female PV may ultimately interfere with the very goals the denial is intended to achieve because, when the evidence finally prevails, the discrepancy could undermine the credibility of the feminist cause. It may alienate young women from the feminist cause, and it could weaken the public base of feminist support. At the same time, casting

PV as almost exclusively a male crime angers men who feel that they are being unjustly accused and provides fuel for the fire of extremist men's groups. These organizations often have a larger antifeminist agenda and publicize feminist denial and distortion of the evidence on PV as part of that larger effort. This is happening in many countries. Finally, I am concerned that the denial in the face of overwhelming evidence may reduce the credibility of feminist scholarship among academics.

Lesbians Are Not Immune to Abusive Relationships

Victoria A. Brownworth

Victoria A. Brownworth, a journalist, author, and editor, teaches writing and film at the University of the Arts in Philadelphia. She is the author of numerous books, among them Day of the Dead.

The night was beautiful—starlit and sultry as only a summer night in the country can be. My lover and I were sitting by the lake. It was picture-postcard romantic.

Until we heard the screams.

We ran toward the sound and found a woman crying, her face bloody. We were at a lesbian retreat with no men on the premises. Who could have done this to her?

The woman told us her girlfriend had hit her repeatedly because another woman had been flirting with her.

That incident happened years ago, yet the details are still fresh in my mind—the screams, the blood, even how the lesbians in charge of the retreat acted as if the victim had brought the beating on herself, insisting to onlookers that it was nothing to be concerned about. That night, the abuser was allowed to stay at the camp because the whole thing was deemed, as it so often is, a she said/she said situation.

The safety of our women-only space was violated—not by a man, but by another woman.

Relationship violence is nothing new, nor is its appearance in the entertainment headlines (Tina Turner, Nicole Brown Simpson, et al.), but the issue led the news again earlier this year when pop stars Rihanna and her longtime boyfriend, Chris Brown, had a fight that resulted in serious injuries to Rihanna and Brown's arrest.

Brown was charged with felony assault. Court documents alleged—and photos that were bandied about the tabloids and the blogosphere seemed to support the claim—that Brown had beaten, punched, bitten and scratched Rihanna while also threatening to kill her.

If blaming women for being beaten seems retrogressive, that's because it is.

The incident led (ever so briefly) to a national discussion about relationship violence, but what that discourse really revealed was even more unsettling.

In 2009, we presume a post-feminist consciousness that has ceased to blame women for the violence against them. And yet, the Rihanna-Brown incident revealed that many women and girls think the Grammy-winner deserved what she got.

On an episode of *Oprah* devoted to the issue, several girls reiterated this position—it was Rihanna's fault, because she allegedly started the argument that led to her beating.

If blaming women for being beaten seems retrogressive, that's because it is. And yet, the prevailing perception—among women as well as men, according to many who work in the domestic violence field—is that young women are both more likely to be victims of relationship violence and also more likely to excuse their perpetrator regardless of his, or her, gender.

Robert L. Hacker, executive director of Philadelphia's Women in Transition—one of the oldest women's service agencies for abused women and the first in the nation to offer a program for battered lesbians—admits that women are in abusive relationships at younger ages, and that young lesbians and bisexual women are facing nearly as much violence as their straight counterparts.

"We have been doing all these programs with younger women," she explains, "and it's just shocking how many teens and women in their 20s are dealing with abuse. For some, it's all they have ever known in a relationship. More stunning still is that it's not just male-female violence. We're seeing more and more abusive relationships among lesbians and bisexual women. It's a very sad trend."

Lesbian Violence Takes Different Forms

Lesbian-lesbian violence is no more anomalous than male-female violence—it just takes different forms, explains Lee Carpenter, the former legal director at Equality Advocates Pennsylvania and an assistant professor at Temple University.

Carpenter handles domestic violence cases and protection-from-abuse orders for LGBT [lesbian, gay, bisexual, and transgender] clients. She also gives workshops on domestic violence, in which she discusses how to combat the most common forms of lesbian domestic violence: harassment, outing and stalking.

A factor unique to LGBT domestic violence victims, according to Carpenter, is a fear that revealing the abusive nature of the relationship to the broader culture will confirm already existing stereotypes of queer relationships as inherently pathological.

"We like to protect our own from outsiders," asserts Carpenter. "We don't want our dirty laundry aired in the straight arena. We don't want to give them reasons to point fingers at us. So we pretend it's all right, even when it isn't."

Carpenter emphasizes that the perception that women don't hurt one another, or that battering is solely a heterosexual crime, adds dramatically to the isolation of lesbians who are in violent relationships. This in turn makes it even harder for them to escape. Many lesbians already feel isolated from their families or friends because their lesbianism is either a secret or a source of contention, Carpenter asserts. Seeking help is all the more difficult under those circumstances.

A Case of Lesbian Battering

Jessica Barnes was one of those women. She did not feel she could ask for help when her girlfriend, Sammy, started to become abusive. (Names have been changed.)

"We met right after I started college," Barnes explained. "I just fell for her immediately. I was so in love. I thought her jealousy was flattering—at first."

Sammy was 20; Barnes, 18 years old.

"The first time she smacked me, I was really surprised," Barnes acknowledged. "She shoved me, then she smacked me. Then she said she was sorry, put her arms around me and kissed me. She didn't really hurt me, so I just let it go."

One of the reasons Barnes said she "let it go" was because she was the butch [mannish or dominant] in the relationship and Sammy was the femme [womanish or submissive].

"I thought it was kind of like with guys hitting girls—if the girl hits back it sort of doesn't count," she explained. "Except I never hit her or shoved her or anything."

The abuse soon became habitual, according to Barnes. "We would go out and she would accuse me of flirting with other women when I wasn't. And then she would shove me or hit me, or both. It became a really regular thing."

Barnes said that the two were living in a small college town in New England, and that made it more difficult for her to imagine telling anyone about the abuse.

"I felt really alone. And I wondered if this was just the way it was. I'd never been in a long-term relationship before. So I thought, maybe this is what happens when lesbians are together."

One night, Sammy shoved Barnes so hard that she fell over a chair and broke her wrist. She was in a cast for eight weeks.

"Suddenly I realized that I really was in an abusive relationship and I needed to get out," Barnes said. "I told her it was over. I changed the locks on my door. I changed my cell number. I changed my email address. She wouldn't leave me alone. I was scared for a long time. She sliced up the tires on my bike. She put cat shit in my mailbox. She told people weird stuff about me that wasn't true. It was so painful. I still loved her, but I was too scared of her to be with her."

Lesbians in abusive relationships have a hard time reaching out, no matter their age, race or class status.

Barnes' experience is far from singular. "There is acculturation about what domestic violence is supposed to look like," Carpenter explains. "It provides an easy out for the batterer: 'I'm not a man. You weren't abused.' It's emotionally crippling for the person being battered. It invalidates the reality of her trauma."

"Lesbians in abusive relationships have a hard time reaching out, no matter their age, race or class status," Hacker adds. "There are stresses on lesbian relationships that just are not present in heterosexual relationships, Homophobia, isolation, self-loathing, the feeling that you only have each other against the outside world—all of these things can play a role in an abusive relationship between two women. They also make it that much harder for women to seek help, or find it."

Despite the increasing awareness of relationship violence, young women continue to fall prey to it. Abusive relationships among teens and young adults has skyrocketed by 40 percent in the past decade. While there are no clear statistics on how many teens are in abusive relationships, the estimate from public health officials is 10 percent. A 2007 Centers for Disease Control survey of 15,000 teens confirmed that 10 percent had experienced physical violence at the hands of a partner.

In January, the *New York Times* detailed a series of initiatives in high schools around the country to help alert students and their parents to the warning signs of "dangerous dating behavior" and what actions are not acceptable or healthy. Some schools are being mandated to teach about abusive dating relationships in grades seven through 12, but they only focus on male-female relationships.

In New York, teens in abusive relationships can file for protection-from-abuse orders just like adults, but through family court rather than criminal court, in an expansion of the domestic violence laws in the state. But new provisions only apply in male-female relationships. A lesbian teen in an abusive relationship with another teen would have no recourse for protection—even it she had the courage to seek it. Other states are considering adopting similar provisions, but, once again, they are likely to neglect the inclusion of a clause for LGBT teens.

The biggest problem for lesbians being battered is acknowledging what's happening.

Isolation Is a Primary Issue

Isolation is a primary issue for queers in abusive relationships—many are isolated already, simply because they are queer. "I just didn't know where to turn," Barnes explains. "There were all these LGBT services on campus, but none of them were for abuse." Barnes said she finally confided in a friend who told her that she couldn't possibly be the one who was abused because "I was the top [dominant one]. That just made it all the harder."

Dr. Jennifer Goldenberg is a clinical social worker who specializes in trauma and has written on the subject. She said that battered women are often convinced that they deserve the abuse that they're getting.

"[The victim] comes to believe that she is the cause of the abuse, that if she just got the dinner on the table faster, if the house wasn't a mess, if whatever, if she had jumped when her partner said 'jump' she would have not gotten the abuse. So she becomes convinced over time that it's her behavior that's causing the abuse. That's not every abuse victim, but it is a pattern that we see in domestic violence situations."

Hacker agrees; "There are so many things a batterer will do to the person he or she is battering. The biggest problem for lesbians being battered is acknowledging what's happening. It's not in your head; it's not any different than if it [were] a man doing this to you, and you do need to leave this abusive person and get help."

Another factor, says Hacker, is even more sinister: "Many women internalize homophobia to such a degree that they are literally trying to beat the queer out of their own partner. Society is certainly to blame for homophobia, but we have to hold batterers accountable."

Carpenter adds that for lesbians who split up after an abusive relationship, lines are often drawn—literally—in the community, "There are certain spaces that lesbians may have to eventually give to a partner, like community spaces, because the community is so small."

The advice for lesbians of any age who are being abused is the same, say the experts and survivors alike: Seek help. It is never OK for someone to shove, slap or hit you. It's never OK for them to isolate you from your friends or force you to have sex, It's never OK for them to say abusive things to you or threaten you with outing.

Hacker adds, "If there is one thing I have said repeatedly to abused women over the years, it's to remember that you are valuable. Abusers try to take your identity, and for lesbians who have struggled harder than most women to find their own identity, this is especially hard."

Today, Barnes is in a new relationship. But she hasn't forgotten what happened between her and Sammy.

"It really warped my view of lesbian relationships," she says. "I was really afraid the first time I had an argument with my new girlfriend, so I told her about what happened with Sammy. She told me she would never hit me, no matter how angry she was. Now I just have to learn to believe it."

Are Efforts to Reduce Family Violence Effective?

Overview: An Integrated Approach Is Needed to Reduce Domestic Violence, Child Abuse, and Youth Violence

Centers for Disease Control and Prevention

The Centers for Disease Control and Prevention (CDC) is a federal public health agency under the US Department of Health and Human Services.

Intimate partner violence (IPV) is a significant public health problem in the United States. Research indicates that IPV exists on a continuum from episodic violence—a single or occasional occurrence—to battering. Battering is more frequent and intensive and involves one partner who develops and maintains control over the other. . . .

All forms of IPV, from episodic violence to battering, are preventable. The key to prevention is focusing on first-time perpetration and first-time victimization. Knowledge about the factors that prevent IPV is lacking. CDC is working to better understand the developmental pathways and social circumstances that lead to this type of violence. In addition, the agency is helping organizations evaluate the effectiveness of existing programs to reduce both victimization and perpetration.

The Domestic Violence Prevention Enhancement and Leadership Through Alliances (DELTA) program seeks to reduce the incidence (i.e., number of new cases) of IPV in funded communities. The program addresses the entire continuum of IPV from episodic violence to battering through a variety of activities.

Centers for Disease Control and Prevention, "Domestic Violence Prevention Enhancement and Leadership Through Alliances (DELTA)," August 16, 2011. CDC.gov.

The Family Violence Prevention Services Act was amended in the 1994 Violent Crime Control and Law Enforcement Act to support the work of Coordinated Community Responses (CCRs) addressing IPV at the local level. Chapter 6 of Title IV (Violence Against Women Act) of the Violent Crime Control and Law Enforcement Act funded nonprofit organizations to sustain IPV intervention and prevention projects (CCRs) in local communities.

CDC began funding the DELTA Program in 2002.

In 2010, the Family Violence Prevention and Services Act was reauthorized. The community demonstration projects were officially replaced with the DELTA name. The reauthorization continues to direct CDC to fund state domestic violence coalitions for the purpose of funding and supporting local efforts to prevent intimate partner violence.

A CCR is an organized effort to prevent and respond to IPV. These efforts can be organized formally (e.g., nonprofit organization) or informally (e.g., group of concerned citizens). CCRs typically involve diverse service sectors (e.g., law enforcement, public health, and faith-based organizations) and populations. Historically, CCRs have focused on providing services to victims, holding batterers accountable, and reducing the number of recurring assaults. Few have concentrated on stopping initial IPV, otherwise known as primary prevention.

CDC was given the responsibility of administering the federal funds provided by this legislation. The monies were first used to fund 10 CCR demonstration projects. To facilitate primary prevention at the community level, CDC began funding the DELTA Program in 2002. Nine state domestic violence coalitions were initially funded; five more were added in 2003.

The federal legislation is intended to support community level efforts. CDC funds state-level domestic violence coalitions to provide prevention-focused training, technical assistance, and funding to local CCRs. A local nonprofit organization serves as the fiscal agent and receives DELTA Program funding to support the local CCR's adoption of primary prevention principles and practices. CCRs integrate prevention strategies through increased cooperation and coordination among participating sectors.

Prevention strategies . . . may include mentoring and peer programs designed to promote intimate partnerships based on mutual respect and trust.

Program Concepts

Primary prevention is the cornerstone of the DELTA Program. Prevention strategies are guided by a set of principles including:

Preventing first-time perpetration and first-time victimization;

Reducing risk factors associated with IPV;

Promoting protective factors that reduce the likelihood of IPV;

Implementing evidence-supported strategies that incorporate behavior and social change theories; and

Evaluating prevention strategies and using results to form future plans.

Prevention requires understanding the circumstances and factors that influence violence. CDC uses a four-level, social ecological model to better understand violence and potential strategies for prevention. This model considers the complex interplay between individual, relationship, community, and societal factors, and allows us to address risk and protective factors from multiple domains.

The DELTA Program encourages the development of comprehensive prevention strategies through a continuum of activities that address all levels of the social ecology. It is important that these activities are developmentally appropriate and are conducted over several life stages. This approach is more likely to prevent IPV across a lifetime than any single strategy or policy change.

Individual-level influences are personal history factors that increase the likelihood of becoming an IPV victim or perpetrator. Examples include attitudes and beliefs that support IPV, isolation, and a family history of violence. Prevention strategies at this level are often designed to promote attitudes, beliefs, and behaviors that support intimate partnerships based on mutual respect and trust. Specific approaches may include education and life skills training.

Relationship-level influences are factors that increase risk because of relationships with peers, intimate partners, and family members. A person's closest social circle peers, partners, and family members influence their behavior, and contribute to their range of experience. Prevention strategies at this level may include mentoring and peer programs designed to promote intimate partnerships based on mutual respect and trust.

The community level of the model examines the contexts in which social relationships are embedded—such as schools, workplaces, and neighborhoods—and seeks to identify the characteristics of these settings that are associated with victims or perpetrators of violence. Prevention strategies at this level are typically designed to impact the climate, processes, and policies in a given system. Social norm and social marketing campaigns are often used to foster community climates that promote intimate partnerships based on mutual respect and trust.

Societal-level influences are larger, macro-level factors, such as gender inequality, religious or cultural belief systems, societal norms, and economic or social policies that influence IPV. Prevention strategies at this level typically involve collaborations by multiple partners to promote social norms, policies, and laws that support gender and economic equality and foster intimate partnerships based on mutual respect and trust.

Current Activities

State domestic violence coalitions that receive DELTA Program funds are working to build IPV prevention capacity within their organization, state, and local communities. Within each DELTA Program state, evaluators are working with the state domestic violence coalitions and local CCRs to assess changes in state and local capacity to prevent IPV and the impact of each CCR's effort to prevent IPV.

Between 2005 and 2009, the 14 state domestic violence coalitions worked with a diverse group of people from within their state to develop a 5–8 year IPV Prevention Plan. For most of these states, this was the first time a primary prevention plan for IPV had been developed. These plans focus on the strategies needed to build the infrastructure required to prevent IPV as well as the strategies needed to prevent first-time perpetration or first-time victimization. Currently, the 14 state domestic violence coalitions are implementing and evaluating these plans. The success, challenges and lessons learned by DELTA Program grantees in developing, implementing and evaluating their state plans will provide a wealth of information to CDC and others on how to develop an IPV primary prevention infrastructure and address IPV to achieve programmatic goals. Each state domestic violence coalition is also working to integrate primary prevention principles into their own operating structures and processes, develop primary prevention resources, and deliver primary prevention training and technical assistance to various partners throughout their state.

At the local level, state domestic violence coalitions are supporting more than 45 local CCRs. The activities of these CCRs are quite diverse due to the differing needs and circumstances of each community: some CCRs are working with schools to prevent teen dating violence, some are working with the faith community to support healthy relationship development, and others are working with men and boys to prevent first-time male perpetration.

By focusing on multiple levels within each state, CDC is supporting comprehensive efforts to prevent IPV. Many believe that IPV is a community problem requiring a community solution.

DELTA PREP Project

DELTA PREP (Preparing and Raising Expectations for Prevention) is a 4-year project funded in 2007 to support an additional 19 state-level domestic violence coalitions and is a collaborative effort between CDC, the CDC Foundation and the project's funder, the Robert Wood Johnson Foundation. DELTA PREP project staff provides training and technical assistance to build DELTA PREP coalitions' organizational capacities to address IPV primary prevention.

With peer coaching support and lessons learned from DELTA coalitions, DELTA PREP coalitions are integrating primary prevention into their organizational structures and partnership work, and building leadership for IPV primary prevention in their states. Through participation in DELTA PREP, state domestic violence coalitions will be better positioned to serve as catalysts for promotion and implementation of primary prevention programs, policies and practices at the state and community levels. Project accomplishments include:

Coalitions have documented over 200 organizational changes to build their coalition's internal capacity for IPV primary prevention work.

Cross-site evaluation using multiple methods and data sources to explore the links between building organizational capacity and engaging in primary prevention activities at the state and community-levels.

Opportunities for shared learning between DELTA PREP and DELTA coalitions, as well as other national partners doing primary prevention work.

Data-to-Action Process Improvement Framework to inform technical assistance, coaching activities, and product development for dissemination.

National Leadership Committee with representatives from federal agencies, national domestic violence groups, academia, public health departments, and prevention practitioners.

Police Officers Can Prevent Repeat Abuse by Directing Victims to Available Services

Rebecca Kanable

Rebecca Kanable is a writer specializing in law enforcement topics.

Studying domestic violence for more than 25 years, Jacquelyn Campbell, Ph.D., of the Johns Hopkins University School of Nursing, found that in 50 percent of domestic violence–related homicides, officers had previously responded to a call where a homicide occurred.

Rarely do victims who may be killed or seriously injured seek help to end the cycle of violence. Campbell's research shows only 4 percent of domestic violence murder victims nationwide had availed themselves to domestic violence intervention services. Yet these services are important. Campbell found that the re-assault of domestic violence victims in high danger was reduced by 60 percent when they went to a shelter.

Handing out print materials that describe domestic violence intervention resources and contact information didn't seem to prompt any action—other than frustrating the officers because victims weren't seeking help.

"There are some domestic situations that just trouble you—you worry something is going to happen to the victim, and there wasn't anything you felt you could do about it," says David Sargent, a retired police officer who's now a consultant and trainer for the Maryland Network Against Domestic Violence (MNADV).

Rebecca Kanable, "Learning to Read the Danger Signs: Maryland Patrol Officers Take an Extra Step to End Domestic Violence Homicides," *Law Enforcement Technology*, v. 37, no. 3, March 2010, p. 8. All rights reserved. Reproduced by permission.

In Maryland and seven other areas of the country, that's changing. Based on Campbell's research, MNADV put together a model program to prevent domestic violence homicides and serious injury by encouraging more victims to seek services offered by domestic violence intervention programs. MNADV's Lethality Assessment Program (LAP) has two parts: the lethality screen for first responders to identify victims with increased risk for homicide; and a protocol to refer victims to services, such as counseling and shelter. All Maryland law enforcement agencies that respond to calls for service use LAP; and in 2009, additional agencies in Florida and Vermont implemented LAP.

The lethality screen helps officers delve deeper to better understand a situation and recognize the danger signs predictive of homicide.

Before officers started using the lethality screen, Officer Erika Heavner of the Howard County Police Department in Maryland [states that] she and other officers primarily focused on "the here and now."

In other words, they were identifying if anyone is injured, or how to resolve the situation at hand.

She says when questioned, a victim might have said little more than, "We argued, he shoved me and left."

The lethality screen helps officers delve deeper to better understand a situation and recognize the danger signs predictive of homicide, or as the LAP information packet says, officers learn to read the danger signs.

Not every victim of domestic violence is screened. Officers initiate a lethality screen when an intimate relationship is involved and:

- An assault is believed to have occurred;

- The potential for danger is high;

- Officers responded to calls involving the victim or location before;

- Or an officer believes an assessment should be conducted.

If a victim resists screening, he or she becomes a lost opportunity.

"We don't know if she's a high-danger victim or not," Sargent says.

If a victim agrees to participate in the screening, 11 yes-or-no questions are asked based on Campbell's work looking at why more than 4,000 victims of domestic violence were killed or nearly killed, and are modeled after Campbell's dangerous assessment instrument for clinical use.

Using a checklist format, officers can consistently obtain the most valuable information.

Questions, for example, include:

- Has he or she ever used a weapon against you or threatened you with a weapon?

- Do you think he or she might try to kill you?

Screening Helped Empathy

Retired Howard County Sgt. Steve Martin, who supervised his department's domestic violence unit, says when officers initially started using the screening tool, they would say, "I can't believe how bad this woman has it."

Overall, Martin found officers trained to use the screening tool became more empathetic to a victim's plight.

After a victim has been identified as a high-danger victim, officers use the LAP protocol. They tell victims that they are in danger. Specifically, an officer may say, "In situations like this, people have been killed."

Next, the officer says, "What I'd like to do now is call the domestic violence hotline so I can get some information to help you. While I'm on the phone, I'd like you to think about speaking with the hotline worker."

Hotline workers have written guidelines to help ensure a victim gets basic information for immediate safety planning, and can even schedule the victim to see a counselor.

Regardless of whether or not the victim says he or she wants to talk to a hotline worker, the officer will call the hotline and provide basic information. If the victim has previously indicated he or she does not want to talk on the phone, the officer again encourages him or her and asks if the victim would like to talk to the hotline worker. If the victim still does not want to talk on the phone, they don't have to. The advocate then provides basic safety planning information that the officer conveys to the victim.

If the victim has said yes, the officer hands the victim the phone. The hotline worker's objective in a brief conversation (no more than 10 minutes) is to encourage the victim to go into domestic violence intervention services. Hotline workers have written guidelines to help ensure a victim gets basic information for immediate safety planning, and can even schedule the victim to see a counselor.

"While we want to be proactive, we want to give the victim information that will empower her to decide to seek help," Sargent says. "It's always the victim who is making the decision. The emphasis in training is on encouraging the victim. The police officer encourages the victim to talk on the phone, and the advocate encourages the victim to go in for services."

Most advocates and officers in Maryland then provide further encouragement and support through follow-up home visits or phone calls.

Realizing the Danger

Research has shown that victims who experience domestic violence early on continue to be victims of abuse through life, thinking that's the norm, Martin points out. They don't think they need help, he adds.

By going through the questions, victims start to realize the danger they are in.

"I think it helps them see—for their sake and for the sake of their kids—they really need to start taking steps to get out of the situation," Heavner says.

Before lethality assessments, Heavner says a victim tended to downplay her situation. She would say something like, "This is just how he is; this kind of stuff has always happened. I just can't get rid of him." The victim wouldn't necessarily come forward with the fact that she was threatened in the past.

Heavner remembers a woman's ex-boyfriend kicking down the woman's door to break into her home when she and her two young daughters were present. He left before police officers arrived on the scene, and they had been to the scene before. Once the victim answered the assessment questions and heard herself verbalize what was really going on, she started thinking about getting a protective order and going forth with charges.

In general, Heavner says victims are more willing to take action because they've been confronted with serious information. . . .

[The Lethality Assessment Program] is an award-winning program.

[Ron] Russum, a retired state trooper, police chief and deputy sheriff, says, "I would encourage every police agency and domestic violence intervention program in the nation to explore how they can make LAP work in their area and implement it when they can. Police can't work without the domestic violence programs, and the programs can't work without the police. They have to work together."

Victims' attitudes are changing, he says. They may have heard that help is available before, but he says it's never been this easy to get help.

LAP is an award-winning program. The Ash Institute for Democratic Governance and Innovation at Harvard [University's] Kennedy School [of Government] named LAP as one of the Top 50 Programs of the 2008 Innovations in American Government Awards competition.

Law enforcement agencies participating in LAP track how many high-danger victims talk to a domestic violence advocate. Maryland's four-year average, from 2006 to 2009, was 59 percent (7,090). Another statistic agencies track is how many victims went into services (for counseling or shelter, for example). Here, the statewide average for the same time span is 30 percent (2,072), which may not seem like a lot, but Sargent reminds that Campbell's research showed only 4 percent of victims at risk of being killed ever sought the help of a domestic service provider. Going beyond the four-year average, Sargent sees this percent increasing. Last quarter [Oct.–Dec. 2009], 37 percent (296 victims) sought help, he says.

"I credit the police officers and the domestic violence advocates on the hotline for doing a better job of getting these victims who are not necessarily ready to get on the phone to go into those services," he says.

Police officers and hotline workers were the first to receive LAP training. MNADV's overall goal is to promote a coordinated community response using LAP.

"We want anyone who might come into contact with a victim to know the signs of lethal danger and be able to do virtually the same thing a police officer does—use the screen, say the same kinds of things to the victim and connect the victim to the local domestic violence intervention provider," Sargent says.

Already he has been working with two hospitals to create a model for health care workers.

Others MNADV looks to include are clergy, legal advocates, social workers, educators, businesses, community groups, family members and the general public.

"Family members may know what's going on but maybe don't know what to do or where to turn," Sargent says. "We want them to know there's a place victims should be encouraged to call. We don't want to create undue alarm, but we want them to understand that they may have a loved one who is in grave danger."

Sargent's team has begun working with two counties in Maryland, so various agencies and organizations throughout the county are doing the LAP through a coordinated community response approach.

Once you start doing LAP, he says, the positive effects start rippling out and educate the entire system.

End the Cycle

MNADV is working to extend the training beyond Maryland's borders. In October 2008, the Department of Justice awarded an Edward Byrne Memorial Grant to MNADV to provide train-the-trainer instruction and technical assistance to law enforcement and community-based domestic violence programs.

Kansas City (Mo.) Police Department is in one of those areas. Police officers responding to calls, taking reports, investigating and making arrests—these things don't break the cycle of violence, says Capt. Mark Folsom, commander of the Kansas City Police Department Special Victims Unit. Law enforcement is just part of the equation, he says. "By involving domestic violence advocates, hopefully we get victims help so the cycle can be broken.

"Our goal is to make a difference in the community by connecting victims to the resources that they need," Folsom says. "Hopefully, that makes a difference for them personally. Hopefully, that makes a difference for us, as a police department, by lowering our crime numbers. And hopefully, that makes the city a safer place to live in."

From June to December 2009, Kansas City did 1216 attempted screens. Of those, 831 were high danger, and 514 of the high-danger victims spoke to a counselor.

"[LAP is] something that at the very minimum tells the victim she's in a dangerous situation," Folsom says. "Maybe that's all it takes for her to change her life and get the help she needs."

The Clergy Can Provide Counseling to Help Women End Abusive Relationships

Charles W. Dahm

Charles W. Dahm is associate pastor of St. Pius V Parish in Chicago and the author of Parish Ministry in a Hispanic Community.

Not long ago Juan and Carmen came to see me to register for the baptism of their third child. I had officiated at their wedding 10 years before. When I asked them how they were getting along, Carmen (whose name, like the other examples in this article, has been changed to protect her privacy) responded, "Well, OK. We have our problems like any other couple."

That was a red flag and, as it turned out, a disguised call for help. I requested to talk to her alone. Amidst a flood of tears she recounted her pain. I asked her if she was suffering physical, emotional, economic, or verbal abuse and asked her to be specific. I learned that she had been hit a number of times and that her husband's verbal and emotional abuse and his control of her life had destroyed her self-confidence and self-esteem. She was a depressed woman without hope.

With her permission I interviewed Juan alone. I confronted him about his abuse, which, to my surprise, he admitted, albeit partially. I invited him to join our men's group to deal with his violent behavior, and I invited Carmen to enter our counseling program and join one of our women's support

Charles W. Dahm, "Let's Stop Ignoring Domestic Violence: It's Time for Parishes to Help Battered Spouses and Their Children Step Out of the Shadows and Get the Assistance They Need," *U.S. Catholic*, v. 76, no. 10, October 2011, p. 27. Reproduced by permission. Subscriptions: $29/year from 205 West Monroe, Chicago, IL 60606; Call 1-800-328-6515 for subscription information or visit www.uscatholic.org.

groups to learn about the dynamics of domestic violence and to grow stronger in dealing with Juan.

Juan failed to follow through with my offer of counseling—only about one in 20 male abusers changes his behavior—but Carmen did. In time she gathered the understanding and strength to confront her husband's abuse, and when he was unwilling to change, Carmen eventually freed herself from her abusive relationship. Now she inspires hope in other women trapped in domestic violence.

Every Fifteen Seconds

Research shows that in the United States every 15 seconds a woman is battered. One of every three women is hit or abused sexually by her partner sometime in her lifetime. During the Vietnam War 58,000 U.S. soldiers died. During that same period 54,000 women were murdered by their partners in the United States. Even worse, women are far more at risk of being beaten when they are pregnant.

Boys who witness domestic violence are twice as likely to abuse their own partners and children when they become adults. Half the men who abuse their female partners also abuse their children. Forty percent of teenage girls ages 14 to 17 report knowing someone their age who has been hit by a boyfriend. Men are also battered, but they account for fewer than 8 percent of all victims.

Domestic violence happens in every parish, community, and economic class, and in every ethnic group. It makes no difference if you are African American, Hispanic, Asian, or Caucasian, rich or poor. And in times of economic or family crisis, the incidence of domestic violence increases.

Many abused women are unaware they are victims because they are in denial or minimize the abuse, excuse their husbands, or don't recognize verbal abuse as violent behavior. When Sheila's brother referred her to me, she was the principal of a large high school and finishing her Ph.D. in education. Although her husband used the foulest of language toward her and had threatened to kill her if she left him (and he had a gun in the house), she still did not perceive herself as a victim of domestic violence.

In their pastoral letter on domestic violence, "When I Call for Help," The U.S. Catholic bishops "state as clearly and strongly as we can that violence against women, inside or outside the home, is never justified." And they draw an important conclusion: "We emphasize that no person is expected to stay in an abusive marriage."

When I began to preach about [domestic violence], more and more women came looking for help.

Although the bishops have urged all clergy and lay ministers to reach out to victims of domestic violence, Catholic parishes and institutions have largely ignored that call. Rarely is domestic violence mentioned in a homily, let alone addressed as the main topic.

Although studies show that women victims would prefer to see their pastor or minister for consolation and direction, they generally do not because they perceive disinterest or lack of understanding of their abuse. When Gabriela came to me, she said her pastor had told her to stay with her husband, pray for his conversion, and try not to upset him.

I was the pastor of St. Pius V in Chicago for eight years before I realized the extent of domestic violence among our parishioners and the need for a ministry to raise awareness about domestic violence and to reach out to its victims. A pastoral counselor opened my eyes to the violence around me.

When I began to preach about it, more and more women came looking for help. Our parish soon decided to expand our services to victims. We successfully sought grants to hire additional counselors. Today, with six full-time counselors, St. Pius V has the largest parish-based program on domestic violence in the country.

When women asked for help for their children, we dedicated one counselor to work with children. Even children who aren't themselves the direct victims of domestic violence are traumatized by witnessing abuse against their mothers. Each year the parish receives about 200 new women clients and nearly 225 new children.

When the women asked us to help their partners, we began offering services to abusers who are not currently violent and who come of their own volition and not by court mandate. Thirty men participate each week in our men's group.

The clients in our parish program are mostly Hispanic immigrant women. We offer them individual counseling, support groups, case management, and court advocacy. There are support groups with child care to accommodate mothers, and there are also support groups for young children and for teens.

Creating a Pastoral Response

Although most parishes are not able to develop as large and comprehensive a program as St. Pius V, parishes can and should create a pastoral response to the victims of abuse in their midst.

To promote greater awareness and to expand parish-based ministry to victims, Chicago Catholics, including several women survivors, organized the Archdiocesan Committee on Domestic Violence. What we ask more parishes to do is simple: Preach about domestic violence at all parish Masses on a weekend and ask people interested in developing a ministry to meet during the following week. Generally 25 to 40 people, including some survivors, attend these sessions to plan further action.

After sharing their experience of domestic violence, the participants discuss ways their parish could mirror Jesus' compassion by being sensitive to victims of domestic violence and providing resources for them. The parish can establish a support group for victims as well as a committee to create awareness. That parish committee then looks for competent people to train parish staff—from receptionists to priests—on how to respond to victims.

The committee can post signs throughout the parish warning against violence and informing victims how to find help. It can identify resources in the area and create a handbook to guide the staff. It can talk to police to learn about their procedures and establish a working relationship with local shelters, counselors, and women's programs.

As a result, domestic violence is no longer a hidden problem but a priority on the parish agenda. All these steps can occur without any major expense.

Women liberated from domestic violence have inspired and enhanced the life of our parish.

In the past two years this model of ministry has been followed in 13 parishes. In Chicago some of these parishes are currently developing a network of mutual support. The commitment of the pastor and his staff coupled with the compassion of parishioners makes this model work.

Once a parish begins to talk about domestic violence and become more sensitive to the problem, more victims begin to come forward. They may be parents in religious education or in the parish school, ministers of communion and catechists, or persons seeking the sacraments of reconciliation, matrimony, or baptism.

Women liberated from domestic violence have inspired and enhanced the life of our parish. They serve in every ministry. By their example and testimony, they teach others about courage, faith, perseverance, and hope. They are grateful for their liberation and eager to give back to the parish. They have been transformed from hidden and marginal members to active ministers serving the community. Their liberation has brought a new beginning—for themselves and for our parish.

The Internet Can Be a Powerful Tool in Combating Family Violence

Elaine M. Chiu

Elaine M. Chiu is professor of law at St. John's University School of Law in New York City.

We have all seen the ads and heard the jingles. Some of us may have even visited the websites. "Come meet your soul mate, come meet your future spouse, come find true love, at Match.com, at eHarmony.com, at Yahoo." Internet dating is a booming business. In 2005, an estimated sixteen million Americans spent more than $245 million looking for love on the Internet. Approximately ten-million Americans are current online daters. In addition to these digital matchmakers, social networking sites like Facebook and MySpace and You Tube offer amazing online communities where folks can advertise their best features. Then, there is Google. Many on the dating circuit use that powerful search engine to find information about a person of interest and swear by Google as an essential resource. Finally, there is an expanding dating-security industry where background check firms will verify age, identity, address, marital status, and criminal history. Some dating sites and social networks have even begun incorporating background checks into their business models. Information is the currency of our time. This fact is true in many aspects of our lives today. It comes as no surprise that it is true in our decisions about love and intimacy, too.

Despite the remarkable reliance on the Internet as a source of information, we have yet to fully take advantage of it in our movement against domestic violence. The movement has been around for a long time now, and it has had an enormous impact on the ways we view domestic violence. Nevertheless, domestic violence continues to occur at worrisome levels and to be a serious problem for our communities. As a result, the movement against domestic violence has reached a stage where its members are hotly debating the success of the changes they have implemented. There is significant disagreement and conflict over whether reforms over the past thirty-five years are working or whether the movement needs to find new approaches.

Information Used as a Weapon

Thus far, information is used as a weapon in the battle against domestic violence in several limited ways. For example, many studies are done on the experiences of domestic violence victims; about the characteristics, backgrounds, and psychiatric profiles of batterers; and on the patterns of violence. Federal and state governments gather lots of statistics on the incidence of domestic violence as reported to or observed by various state actors. They also collect data on the types of interventions states use to respond to domestic violence. Information also appears in awareness campaigns and public service announcements in schools, libraries, hospitals, on billboards, in print media, in television, and on the radio. These publicity efforts educate the public about how to recognize the signs of domestic violence and about the public resources available to help those who are being battered and those who want to stop battering. Lastly, state actors share information about the troubled families experiencing violence in their communities. Their collaboration leads to coordinated monitoring and assistance for these violent families in trouble.

Yet there is still more we can do with information and, specifically, the Internet in combating domestic violence. The Scarlet Letter proposal seeks to empower potential victims of domestic violence with information so that they themselves can make choices that will avoid years of suffering and abuse.

When a person meets someone attractive, and with whom she is contemplating a romantic, intimate relationship, she can access the state data registries to see if that person has ever had a final order of protection issued against him.

The idea is to allow public access to the data registries maintained by state governments that contain the identities of the batterers who either are or have been the subjects of final orders of protection. Today almost all fifty states have such data registries in place. In some of them, public access already exists, albeit usually with certain restrictions; in other states, there is no public access at all. The novelty of the idea is not in the compilation and storage of the information; rather, the uniqueness of the proposal is its call to expand access and to publicize widely the fact of such access as a way to reduce the future incidence of domestic violence.

Expanding access unleashes the potential of information as a preemptive weapon. When a person meets someone attractive, and with whom she is contemplating a romantic, intimate relationship, she can access the state data registries to see if that person has ever had a final order of protection issued against him. She can do this search alongside the more familiar Internet tools of Google, MySpace and Facebook with the same purpose of finding out more information about the person of interest. The hope is that if she discovers that such person is subject to a final order of protection, she can then preclude any further interactions with that person to avoid being a future victim of intimate partner abuse. Armed with information, hopefully she chooses not to pursue a romantic relationship in her own self-interest.

This proposal is inspired by several different developments in American society and in criminal law, including the increasing use of the Internet to gain information and form judgments about others. The proposal also calls for the criminal justice system to function as a system that not only punishes but also empowers. It does so by using the Internet to expand and deepen the reach of public condemnation and to be more specific in its condemnation. Enhanced public condemnation will deter more tendencies toward violence and provide greater incentives to rehabilitate. Most importantly, it will reduce intimate violence. By doing so, the proposal addresses the stagnancy of the domestic violence movement, particularly in the massive infrastructure states have built upon orders of protection. Building on these trends, this proposal warrants further examination. . . .

Description of the Scarlet Letter Proposal

Once an order of protection is issued, many states record its issuance in a database. The database might be a special database created for orders of protection or the database can be the state's criminal history database used for all crimes including domestic violence. As a general matter, public access to the specialized databases either does not exist or exists in very limited form. . . .

Operationally, the Scarlet Letter proposal then is fairly simple: to make selective information from the Registry available to the public, along with the information already available from the criminal history records. The public will be able to access the identities of the abusers who received a final order of protection from any court at any time. It would not matter if the final order was issued by a criminal court or a civil court or if the order lasted for five years, three years, or two years. The only requirement is that it is a final order of protection. The reason for this is the greater procedural rigor of final orders over temporary orders. The proposal would not make accessible to the public the identities of the parties in whose protection the orders were issued. This would be kept inaccessible or secret. The database should be searchable by full name along with a date of birth. These search terms are in line with how many open states, including New York, currently allow searches on their criminal history databases. . . .

Many batterers will batter again.

During the past three decades, we have learned a great deal from the many studies about violent families. One powerful observation is that violent families vary widely in their composition, in the frequency of their abuse, in the intensity of the violence, in the pattern of their fighting, in their economic and social characteristics, in their educational backgrounds, etc. Although Dr. Lenore Walker's work on the battered women syndrome is the most broadly known theory, it is far from being the only one and for many violent families, it is far from accurate.

At the risk of essentializing all violent families to one model, I set forth two recurring observations that we see in many (although not all) violent families and relationships. The first observation is that many batterers will batter again. The second observation is that when the violence or abuse first occurs, and then at each subsequent abusive incident, couples are often already in a close and entangled relationship. The dependencies and emotions of such relationships make it extremely difficult to exit the relationships. These two observations combine to make domestic violence such a difficult social problem to solve. The Scarlet Letter proposal is unlike many other past reforms because its potential lies in working within these realities and not against them.

Tremendous Predictive Value

Knowing the identities of individuals who have been subjected to a final order of protection is only helpful if that information has a predictive value. Because the truth is that a high proportion of batterers abuse victims over and over, there is tremendous predictive value.

The phrases repeat batterers and serial batterers describe abusers who engage in two distinct phenomena. Repeat batterers are those abusers who keep abusing their victims, even though they have already been the subject of legal actions, whether civil or criminal, for their behavior toward those victims. Repeat battering is also known as reabuse. Serial batterers are abusers who have multiple victims. They batter more than one person with whom they are intimate or romantically involved. Serial batterers can commit such abuse serially, meaning they move from one victim to the next and, thus, are only abusing one victim at a time. In actuality though there are "serial" batterers who abuse multiple victims at the same time. They would still be categorized as "serial" batterers in studies.

An abuser can be either a repeat or a serial batterer or both or neither. The two categories are not mutually exclusive. For example, Adam can physically attack and emotionally torment Beatrix, and Beatrix can go into court and obtain a civil restraining order against Adam. If Adam continues to emotionally and physically abuse Beatrix, despite the issuance of the order, then he is a repeat batterer. If he also batters another victim, Cindy, at the same time he is battering Beatrix, or shortly thereafter, he is also a serial batterer.

Many batterers are repeat batterers. This has been well-documented by numerous studies. Its incidence is not questioned; instead, what continues to stir controversy are the predictors of reabuse.

Numerous studies have examined individual level characteristics, including demographics and criminal history, interpersonal variables about the nature of the relationship between the batterer and the victim, and systemic variables that cover myriad ways a batterer and victim may engage with the legal system.

In contrast to repeat battering, serial battering has received much less empirical and scholarly attention.

The results of these studies are inconclusive and not helpful as to the exact causes of repeat battering. For instance, in 2000, Professors [Robert J.] White and [Edward W.] Gondolf published a paper that allegedly confirmed that most men who recidivate exhibit dysfunctional personality types, but then in 2001, the same two professors published a second article stating that the causal connection between recidivisim and psychopathic tendencies is more attenuated than first conceived.

In contrast to repeat battering, serial battering has received much less empirical and scholarly attention. In my days as an assistant district attorney prosecuting domestic violence cases, I often heard about serial batterers from their victims. Many women would tell me about the day they finally met their abuser's ex-wife or ex-girlfriend and how they learned that he had actually battered and abused them, too, in much the same way. Specially trained domestic violence police officers at the local precincts would describe their familiarity with the abuse patterns of certain batterers because of the revolving door of victims who would be hurt by them.

The Massachusetts Office of the Commissioner of Probation has conducted two studies that provide some statistical evidence of serial battering. In the first study, they looked at the identities of the offenders and victims of all restraining orders issued for intimate violence from 1992 to 1998 and found that almost one out of every four offenders had two or more unrelated victims. One serial batterer had as many as eight different victims over a six-year period. This first study noted that these offenders either victimized more than one person at a time or moved serially from one victim to the next, and so on. A second study released in 2004 looked at all the restraining orders that were issued in 1998 and followed the criminal history of those offenders thereafter. This study produced even more alarming numbers. Some 43% of these offenders had two or more victims who were unrelated in their history of civil restraining orders. Anywhere from one out of four batterers to two out of five batterers are serial batterers with multiple victims.

Serial Battering "More Interesting"

For the purposes of the Scarlet Letter proposal, the phenomenon serial battering is more interesting than repeat battering. Serial battering supports the view that abuse goes beyond simply interpersonal factors or the interaction between two particular people. It suggests that abusers themselves have certain demographics, personalities, afflictions, or problems that they carry around as they move from one romantic partner to the next. What is most appalling about these stories and statistics, though, is the ease with which serial batterers move from one victim to the next to the next in the status quo. As abuse victims told me again and again in my days as a state prosecutor, they often had no idea about the history of battering and were completely unsuspecting when they decided to get involved with their abusers. Some eventually communicated with former wives, partners, or girlfriends of their batterers and shared the similarities in their experiences of violence and abuse by the same batterer. However, these conversations happened too late.

What do I mean by too late? Consider the standard definition of domestic violence: emotional, physical, and psychological abuse and violence that takes place within the context of a physically intimate relationship. In many instances, this physically intimate relationship is based on emotional love or at least emotional affection. These relationships start off without any abuse. This initial violence-free period can be thought of as an incubation period or probationary period in the relationship.

> *A permanent end to the [abusive]relationship will frequently require formal legal actions.*

What triggers the end of this period is often a change of circumstances. The change typically represents several things: a source of stress to the abuser, a symbolic loss of control for the abuser, and also a deepening bond or commitment of the victim to the abuser. Classic examples of such triggers include marriage and pregnancy.

Both empirical studies and anecdotal evidence show that many victims are first abused on their wedding nights or during their honeymoon. There are numerous accounts of victims being hit for the first time during a pregnancy. Once married or pregnant, victims often have deep emotional ties to the abuser. In addition, there are other concomitant bonds between them, including serious financial dependencies, extended family relationships, and sometimes reliance on one another for lawful immigration status. After marriage, pregnancy, and the birth of children in common, it is no longer easy to leave your abuser. A permanent end to the relationship will frequently require formal legal actions, such as divorce or a child support and custody actions in family court.

The Scarlet Letter proposal intervenes before these triggering events, before the formation of these complicated bonds, and before the difficult exit options. Information will be available to the public at all times, including during the incubation period in those very early moments of a budding relationship, so that individuals can learn about the battering history of their potential romantic partners. If they were to learn of a troubling past record, the individuals can then decide not to pursue the relationships any further. At these early moments, there are no deep ties to stand in the way of relatively easy exits. Public access to order of protection databases then is a powerful preventive measure to reduce the incidence of domestic violence. . . .

The State's Obligation to Protect Citizens

The impact of this proposal will be significant on several different levels. First, the number of individuals whose identities would be included in the database will be quite high. As mentioned above in the New York State example, as of 2006, the total number of orders of protection in the New York State Registry was 1,411,264. This number includes both temporary and final orders of protection and does not distinguish between them; thus, it is hard to know exactly how many final orders of protection there would be in the publicly accessible database. However, with a total of over a million restraining orders, it is certain that the publicly accessible database will have hundreds of thousands of names.

Secondly, the Scarlet Letter proposal will change the direction of the domestic violence movement. Instead of being reactive to past acts of violence, the proposal is preemptive and strives to avoid violence and abuse in the first place. This alone could be a huge reduction in the amount of physical, emotional, and sexual harm suffered by victims of domestic violence. Instead of forcing victims to live with undesirable consequences, such as the potential imprisonment of their batterers, the proposal leaves victims in control. Respect for the autonomy of victims is a feature of libertarian paternalism and critical to acceptance of the proposal by potential victims. In addition, the proposal bridges the gap between those in the domestic violence movement who continue to support the legal approach and those who want to dismantle that approach. The proposal builds upon the existing legal structures of the restraining order regime, but does so in a way that does not add to legal penalties or mandates. Instead, publicly accessible databases operate in that space between public law and private action. This space is typically very difficult to negotiate, but this proposal ambitiously tries.

The final momentum of the proposal lies in its goal to shift the way that society and individual victims think about how to combat domestic violence. Many of the earlier reforms of the domestic violence movement have increased and enhanced the options that individual victims have to try and end the violence in their lives. However, these reforms largely asked the victims to take action themselves to take advantage of their benefits. The state and other individuals, such as prosecutors and social workers and counselors would be there to help but only after violence and abuse have already occurred and only after deep bonds have already formed between the victims and their batterers. The heart of the Scarlet Letter proposal is the collective sharing of information among past, present, and future victims of domestic violence and, in a sense, relies on the ethos of women helping each other. Critically then, the proposal asks the state to join this community effort and facilitate the distribution of information by opening up its existing databases.

One Last Provocative Thought

I want to close this initial discussion of the Scarlet Letter proposal with one last provocative thought. Not only is the Scarlet Letter proposal a good idea, but because the state knows of the strong likelihood of serial battering and knows the identities of past batterers, the state has an obligation to share that information with its citizens. Keeping such information from citizens is ultimately dangerous and unjustified. The state exists to protect the health and safety of its citizens and, many of its female citizens still suffer from the wrath of domestic violence. It is time for the state to face its obligations and to empower its citizens to protect themselves.

Substance Abuse Programs Are Only Marginally Effective in Preventing Child Abuse

Brenda Smith and Mark F. Testa

Brenda Smith is an associate professor in the School of Social Work at the University of Alabama, and Mark F. Testa is the director of the Children and Family Research Center and a professor in the School of Social Work at the University of Illinois, Urbana-Champaign.

For much of the past century of U.S. public involvement in the protection and care of abused and neglected children, the problem of parental alcohol and other drug abuse (AODA) was hidden, at least from the public's eye. . . .

Several trends during the mid-1980s and 1990s helped to bring about greater public awareness of the AODA connection to child maltreatment and foster care. The first was the change in the gender profile of users from disproportionately males and fathers to increasingly females and mothers. Public officials may have been able to turn a blind eye when it was mostly fathers who returned home drunk or stoned; it was quite another matter when female caregivers increasingly numbered among the users.

Second, the spread of illicit drugs, particularly "crack" cocaine in inner-city neighborhoods, alarmed public officials, who predicted dire consequences for crime, welfare dependency, and public health. Even though the detrimental effect of fetal alcohol syndrome had been well established, the uncertain effects of intrauterine exposure of infants to cocaine, heroin, and other hard drugs prompted hospital officials to

Brenda Smith and Mark F. Testa, "Prevention and Drug Treatment," *The Future of Children*, v. 19, no. 2, Fall 2009, p. 147. All rights reserved. Reproduced by permission.

increase the number of toxicology screenings at birth. In some states, a positive finding from such a test provided sufficient grounds for filing a child abuse report.

Between 6 million and 9 million children live in households in which a caregiver abuses alcohol or drugs.

Finally, the shift from a "rights" to a "norms" perspective in federal and state income assistance and child welfare programs helped to enlarge the scope of public interest beyond a narrow focus on child safety to a more diffuse concern with parental responsibility and child well-being in general. Although it is arguable whether parental substance abuse provides a legitimate basis in its own right for protective intervention and child removal, the greater acceptance of government's role in enforcing mainstream parental fitness standards has enlarged the scope of public interest in AODA as a child welfare concern. . . .

The prevalence of children's exposure to parental AODA refers to the proportion of abused and neglected children who are affected by parental alcohol and other drug use at a given time. Estimates vary depending on the definition of AODA used to classify cases, the segment of the child population examined, and the method of data collection used to count the cases. Prevalence estimates are best generated through carefully conducted studies using uniform definitions that rely on samples of cases drawn at random or using some other statistically valid method of selection to generate an estimate within some margin of error, for example, plus or minus a few percentage points. . . .

These prevalence estimates suggest that between 6 million and 9 million children live in households in which a caregiver abuses alcohol or drugs. These numbers far exceed the number of children who become involved in the child welfare system for any reason. Of the approximately 900,000 children with substantiated maltreatment allegations of any kind in 2005, about 300,000 (33 percent) were placed in foster care, leaving about 600,000 children with substantiated allegations at home with their parents. Even if all of these substantiated cases with children in the home involved parental substance abuse, the number would conservatively reflect only about 10 percent of the estimated number of children living with a parent who abuses substances. . . .

Increased Risk of Maltreatment?

Selective prevention, as distinct from universal prevention, refers to interventions that target groups that exhibit above-average risks, such as children exposed to parental AODA. Several studies document a link between parental AODA and child maltreatment, particularly neglect. However, establishing a causal relationship between parental substance abuse and child maltreatment is difficult. . . .

In a rigorous study that is among the few prospective studies to assess the risk of child maltreatment among parents who abuse substances, Mark Chaffin and several colleagues followed for one year parents from a community sample. The researchers compared parents identified as having a substance use disorder and parents without a substance use disorder in self-reports of child maltreatment. Parents with a substance use disorder were three times more likely than those without one to report the onset of child abuse or neglect within the one-year follow-up period. About 3 percent of parents with a substance abuse problem reported child abuse or neglect within the year compared with 1 percent of parents without a substance abuse problem. The researchers found that the influence of substance abuse on maltreatment was maintained even when the parents being compared were similar with respect to such characteristics as parental depression, obsessive-compulsive disorder, household size, age, race, marital status, and socioeconomic status.

The Chaffin study is rigorous and convincing. It offers the best type of evidence for demonstrating a link between substance abuse and child maltreatment. And similar patterns are found in repeated studies that control for other co-existing risk factors. Such studies, however, cannot rule out the possibility that other co-factors associated with substance abuse, such as parental depression, social isolation, or domestic violence, are more directly responsible for higher maltreatment rates. Targeting interventions on a "spurious" association between drug use and maltreatment without attending to the underlying direct causes of both will be ineffectual. . . .

The links between parental substance abuse and child maltreatment surely warrant further study.

The role of substance abuse in increasing risks for child maltreatment will become clearer as researchers succeed in identifying exactly what it is that explains the link between parental substance abuse and child maltreatment. Researchers have proposed a range of potential explanations.

For example, substance abuse may strain social support relationships, leading to social isolation and heightening the risks that family, friends, and neighbors will refrain from lending a hand or stepping in when child-rearing problems arise. Substance abuse may promote impulsivity or reduce parental capacity to control anger under stressful situations. Substance abuse may also distract parents from meeting children's needs or impair their ability to supervise them. The links between parental substance abuse and child maltreatment surely warrant further study because different causal mechanisms call for different ways to conceptualize the problem and determine how to intervene. As one example, different substances may have different consequences for parenting and child safety. The ways in which a sedative, such as alcohol, impairs parenting or threatens child safety could be quite dif-

ferent from the ways in which a stimulant, such as metham-
phetamine, impairs parenting and threatens child safety. Perhaps child safety will be promoted most effectively by
specifically targeted interventions for different types of substance abuse. Likewise, different mechanisms may explain different pathways to child neglect and physical abuse, or mechanisms may differ in different social or economic contexts.

Targeting Families for Treatment

Indicated prevention involves screening abuse and neglect
cases for signs of parental substance abuse to promote sobriety and prevent the recurrence of maltreatment. To date, usual
caseworker practices have not proved effective in identifying
AODA problems among families in the child welfare system
or in preventing subsequent maltreatment allegations once
families are investigated for child maltreatment. An analysis
using data collected on families reported for child maltreatment as part of the National Survey of Child and Adolescent
Well-Being (NSCAW) found that among at-home caregivers
who screened positive for past-year alcohol abuse or illicit
drug use, only 18 percent were identified by caseworkers as
having a substance abuse problem. Among at-home caregivers
meeting criteria for alcohol or drug dependency, caseworkers
identified a substance abuse problem for only 39 percent.
Such findings are consistent with other research indicating
that child welfare caseworkers are ill-equipped to identify substance abuse problems.

When substance abuse is indicated, evidence also casts
doubt that CPS [Child Protective Services] is effective in linking parents to substance abuse services and treatment. A study
focusing on parents with substance abuse problems involved
with child welfare services found that about half received
substance abuse treatment; 23 percent were offered treatment but did not receive it; and 23 percent were not offered
treatment. . . .

Concerted efforts to link clients with treatment sometimes fall short of the goal of preventing subsequent maltreatment, either because of problems with program attendance or because of the nature of the services provided.

Researchers speculate that child welfare caseworkers may rely too heavily on indications of caregiver treatment compliance.

Barbara Rittner and Cheryl Davenport Dozier studied a sample of children with maltreatment allegations who either remained at home under court supervision or were placed with relatives. In about half the cases, a caregiver was mandated by the courts to attend substance abuse treatment. After rating the caregivers for treatment compliance and tracking the cases for eighteen months, the researchers found no correlation between caregivers' treatment compliance and subsequent child maltreatment.

In the researchers' view, the findings raise questions about whether mandated treatment can prevent subsequent maltreatment and whether the treatment is of sufficient quality to help parents. Reflecting on the study findings, the researchers speculate that child welfare caseworkers may rely too heavily on indications of caregiver treatment compliance and give too little attention to family functioning and other indicators of child safety. . . .

Uncertainties about whether substance abuse treatment services can prevent subsequent maltreatment are also reinforced by a series of studies using data from the National Study of Child and Adolescent Well-Being (NSCAW) involving children reported to CPS who remained at home. Aware that the apparent benefits of treatment can often reflect the characteristics of the clients who access, enter, and attend treatment rather than the net effects of the services received, researchers matched caregivers according to characteristics that indicated a need for substance abuse treatment using propensity score methods. Among in-home caregivers matched on need for treatment, those who received treatment services were more likely than those who did not to incur a subsequent maltreatment report within the next eighteen months. In addition, children of the in-home caregivers who received treatment had lower well-being scores than children of caregivers who did not receive treatment. Questions raised by such perplexing findings are further discussed below.

Promoting Family Reunification

Failure to engage parents in drug recovery services or to prevent the recurrence of maltreatment will usually precipitate the children's removal from parental custody and placement into foster care. In these circumstances, attention turns to encouraging or compelling parents to attain sobriety or total abstinence so that the children can safely be restored to their care. The shock of child removal is thought to provide a sufficient incentive for parents to engage in treatment to avoid permanent separation from their children through continued state custody or termination of parental rights. . . .

In an effort to boost reunification rates among children taken from substance-involved parents, the Illinois Department of Children and Family Services secured federal permission to fund a randomized controlled trial of a state-funded enhanced services program that previous quasi-experimental findings suggested showed promise.

Parents whose only problem was substance abuse achieved a 21 percent reunification rate.

The Illinois demonstration was initially implemented in Cook County (which includes the city of Chicago) in April 2000. The demonstration randomly assigned Illinois Performance-Based Contracting agencies to treatment and comparison conditions. Parents were referred on a rotational basis to these agencies and subsequently screened for drug abuse problems. Eligible parents assigned to the comparison condition received the standard substance abuse services. Those assigned to the treatment condition received the standard services plus a package of enhanced services coordinated by a "recovery coach." The recovery coach worked with the parents, child welfare caseworker, and AODA treatment agency to remove barriers to drug treatment, engage the parents in services, provide outreach to re-engage the parent if necessary, and provide ongoing support to the parent and family throughout the permanency planning process. . . .

An investigation by Jeanne Marsh and several colleagues found that although completing at least one level of treatment helped to boost reunification rates, only 18 percent of participants in the Illinois demonstration completed all levels of treatment. Furthermore, besides substance abuse, participants faced other serious problems, such as domestic violence, housing, and mental illness. Only 8 percent of participants had no other problem besides substance abuse; 30 percent had at least one other problem; 35 percent had two other problems; and 27 percent had three or more.

Parents whose only problem was substance abuse achieved a 21 percent reunification rate, while parents with one or more other problems achieved only an 11 percent rate. Reunification rates were highest among the 5 percent of participants who completed mental health treatment (41 percent) and next highest among the 10 percent of participants who solved their housing problems (12 percent). Of the 18 percent of participants who completed all levels of drug treatment, only 25 percent regained custody of their children. The authors concluded that a service integration model designed to increase access to substance abuse treatment will not successfully promote reunification unless outreach and retention services can ensure client progress in the three co-occurring problem areas as well as in completing substance abuse treatment. . . .

Substance-Exposed Infants

As noted, two decades ago Illinois became one of the first states to make the presence of illegal drugs in newborns prima facie [immediate] evidence of abuse and neglect. It enacted legislation that expanded the definition of abused or neglected minors to include newborns whose blood, urine, or meconium [first stool] contained any amount of a controlled substance or its metabolites. The mandate helped to fuel a rise in the number of SEI [substance-exposed infant] reports that peaked at 20 per thousand births in fiscal year 1994. More than 90 percent of reported SEI cases were subsequently indicated for maltreatment because a positive toxicology report meets the credible evidence standard that abuse or neglect has occurred. The proportion of substance-exposed infants who were taken immediately into protective custody (PC) lagged behind the steep rise in reports and hit its highest point in 1999 with 41 percent of reports triggering the state's removal of the infant at birth. Currently the proportion of protective custodies hovers around 33 percent of SEI reports. The risk of removal, however, does not end with the child's birth. Substance-exposed infants run a high risk of being placed in foster care throughout their early childhood. . . .

In the spring of 2008, the *Chicago Tribune* ran a story about a recent graduate of Morehouse College under the headline: "Proof Positive of Flawed Data." It told the story of a Rhodes Scholarship finalist who was born substance-exposed at the start of the SEI epidemic in Chicago in 1986, "among a wave of inner-city babies exposed to crack in their mother's womb, children written off by much of society as a lost generation doomed to failure." The article asserted that the drug panic was fueled by flawed data that warned of neurologically damaged and socially handicapped children that would soon flood the nation's schools and, later on, its prisons.

More recent opinion has backed away from such dire predictions. Much of the earlier work failed to consider the myriad of adverse social, environmental, and other factors that confound the association between parental substance use and impaired childhood growth and development.

No particular set of symptoms supports the popular notion of a "crack baby" syndrome.

Barry Lester was among the first researchers to note that early studies of substance-exposed infants over estimated the effects of cocaine exposure by attributing to cocaine adverse effects that were probably related to other influences such as multiple-drug use, poverty, or cigarette smoking. The challenges associated with identifying specific effects of prenatal cocaine exposure, along with the wide-ranging findings of research on the topic, led a group of leading researchers, including Lester, to argue publicly that no particular set of symptoms supports the popular notion of a "crack baby" syndrome. They asked the media to stop using the stigmatizing term.

Recently, however, Lester has noted that some well-designed studies that control for a range of influences are identifying some apparent effects of prenatal cocaine exposure that may even increase over time. The studies suggest that prenatal cocaine exposure may have neurological effects that become visible only when "higher level demands are placed on the child's cognitive abilities." Lester argues that just as it was initially a mistake to overstate the effects of prenatal cocaine exposure, it would also be a mistake to overlook potential effects that are still largely unknown and warrant further research. . . .

Finding Safe Homes for Kids

Both personal accounts and the best research evidence indicate that finding a safe and lasting home for children born substance-exposed is critical to their healthy development and well-being. As of December 2007, however, only 39 percent of children assigned to the treatment group under the Illinois AODA demonstration had exited from foster care, compared with 36 percent in the comparison group. Not only does this small, albeit statistically significant, difference raise concerns about the advisability of heavily investing in recovery coach services, it raises additional questions about the permanency needs of the remaining 61 to 64 percent of drug-involved children who are still in foster care. Because the average age of children born substance-exposed who are removed from parental custody is less than three, it should not be too challenging to find them permanent homes with relatives either as guardians or as adoptive parents or with foster parents who are willing to become their adoptive parents. Although it is unwise to set too firm guidelines, it strikes us as sensible to set a six-month timetable for parents to engage in treatment and twelve to eighteen months to show sufficient progress in all identified problem areas (presuming that both engagement and progress are determined with fair and valid measures). Thereafter, permanency plans should be expedited to place the child under the permanent guardianship of a relative caregiver or in the adoptive home of a relative, foster parent, or other suitable family. As regards the birth of another substance-exposed infant, it seems reasonable, assuming the availability of services, to initiate alternative permanency plans for all of the children unless the parent demonstrates sufficient progress in all problem areas within six months of the latest child's birth.

In light of the difficulty of isolating the direct effects of prenatal substance abuse and the most recent evidence that some detrimental effects of intrauterine substance exposure on child development may increase over time, the newest empirical findings on the efficacy of Illinois' recovery coach model in decreasing births of substance-exposed infants helps to bolster the case for improved treatment and service coordination regardless of whether intrauterine substance exposure is considered a form of child maltreatment in its own right. Preventing another potential risk to future child well-being, even if parental substance abuse and intrauterine substance exposure prove not to be determinative of child maltreatment directly, seems well worth the cost of investing in parental recovery from substance abuse and dependence. Such efforts, however, should not substitute for a comprehensive approach that addresses the myriad of social and economic risks to child well-being beyond the harms associated with parental substance abuse.

Domestic Violence Programs Are Ineffective and Sometimes Harmful

SAVE: Stop Abusive and Violent Environments

SAVE: Stop Abusive and Violent Environments is an advocacy organization whose mission is to find solutions to domestic violence for victims and their families.

Domestic violence is an important social problem in our country. Two milestones in the national effort to combat intimate partner assault were the enactment of the Family Violence Prevention and Service Act in 1984 and the Violence Against Women Act [VAWA] in 1994. Now, the federal government expends over $1 billion annually to curb partner abuse.

But a broad range of groups—policymakers, service providers, victims' rights organizations, taxpayers, and others—are now asking, Are these programs having their intended effect? Are they working to curb domestic violence?

A range of opinions has been expressed. Representatives of domestic violence shelters often point to an increase in requests for assistance as evidence the problem of intimate partner violence has deteriorated. One Department of Justice official expressed this less-than-sanguine view:

> "We have no evidence to date that VAWA has led to a decrease in the overall levels of violence against women."
> —Angela Moore Parmley, PhD

So the question needs to be posed: Are domestic violence levels currently increasing, remaining steady, or decreasing?

Community surveys, homicide statistics, and reports of non-fatal victimizations all point to the same conclusion: domestic violence rates have followed a pronounced downward trend since the mid-1970s.

Community surveys conducted in 1975 to 1992 reveal a decrease in annual partner aggression rate over that period of time:

- Male victims: From 11.6% to 9.5% of couples

- Female victims: From 12.1% to 9.1% of couples

FBI statistics of intimate partner homicides reveal a substantial decline.

And reports of *non-fatal* victimization paint a similar picture. . . .

Violence Against Women Fell

[Over] a 10-year period, violent crime against women fell at almost identical rates, regardless of the offender type:

- Stranger—52%

- Intimate partner—55%

- Friend or acquaintance—63% . . .

All types of violent crime—robberies, simple assaults, and aggravated assaults—have been on the decline since the early 1980s.

Within that context, this Special Report reviews the evidence regarding the impact of domestic violence programs. Specifically, the Report analyzes the effectiveness of four key violence-reduction strategies widely employed by domestic violence programs:

1. Treatment Services

2. Restraining Orders

3. Mandatory Arrest

4. No-Drop Prosecution

Treatment Services

The dynamics of domestic violence are varied and complex. Partner aggression is influenced by factors such as marital status, age, socio-economic level, drug and alcohol use, psychological disorders, and childhood abuse experiences. Treatment services should be based on a careful client needs assessment, sound scientific research, and the best practices of the counseling profession.

A key factor in the treatment of partner abuse is whether the physical aggression is mutual. Studies typically reveal that at least half of all abuse is reciprocal and initiated by males and females at similar rates. For example, one Centers for Disease Control survey of adults 18–28 years old found that half of all partner violence was reciprocal. Another survey of dating couples reported that 70% of all physical abuse was mutual. Logic dictates that counseling for both partners would be essential for a successful resolution of the conflict.

But ironically, domestic violence treatment standards often discourage family therapy. In 30 states that have implemented standards for offender treatment programs, 42% of those states prohibit couples counseling.

These restrictions have become a point of contention between traditional mental health providers and abuse intervention providers. . . .

Couples therapy has been shown to be effective in treating violent partners. But by policy or by law, domestic violence programs often bar the use of such services.

The 1,200 abuse shelters currently in operation in the United States are considered the mainstay of treatment services for victims of abuse. But what happens inside the protective walls of these facilities?

Feminist therapists advocate that women in shelters should be counseled to view their predicament as a consequence of patriarchy. One national survey found that 45% of shelters viewed their main role as promoting feminist political activism, while only 25% focused on providing treatment and support for abused women.

Today's treatment denies the possibility that women can be violent.

Although researchers have been studying women's shelters for more than 20 years, the quality of the studies has been poor and the findings inconclusive. Such analyses typically lack pre-intervention data or comparison groups and fail to take into account critical control variables.

One early study suggested that shelter residence could trigger new incidents of abuse. But overall, we do not know whether shelter services are effective, benign, or might make the situation worse.

Women are as likely as men to engage in partner aggression. Fewer than one in five cases of female violence are justified by the need for women to act in self-defense. Female-initiated violence is a cause for concern not only because of the physical and psychological effects on her partner, but also because it raises the specter of retaliatory aggression.

So when abusive women request help from domestic violence agencies, they may discover that requests for treatment are dismissed ("He must have done something to provoke you") or that female-specific services are simply non-existent.

For example, one evaluation revealed that among New York City intervention programs, there are "very few that accept female batterers." As attorney Linda Kelly explains, "Today's treatment denies the possibility that women can be violent."

Persons have decried the lack of services for women:

- Researcher Susan Steinmetz tells of receiving letters from violent women who recognized that they needed help, but were "turned away or offered no help when they called a crisis line or shelter."

- Ellen Pence, founder of the Duluth Domestic Abuse Intervention Project, has highlighted the neglect of female abusers: "In many ways, we turned a blind eye to many women's use of violence, their drug use and alcoholism, and their often harsh and violent treatment of their own children."

Darlene Hilker of Florida assaulted her husband. "I grabbed my husband's genitals—that's what I was arrested for," she later admitted. In 2006, the judge ordered her to attend the Women Who Batter program, one of the first such programs ever established in the United States.

Lack of Services for Males

The lack of services for male victims of domestic violence is well documented. One survey of 26 domestic violence shelters in California confirmed the fact that, "Most shelters do not admit males."

Psychologist David Fontes has observed that "if a male victim happens to show up at a domestic violence center, they may try to help him, but are unlikely to have an active outreach program or services specifically set up with his needs in mind." In 2002, Ray Blumhorst contacted 10 shelters in southern California to request help. All 10 shelters turned him down.

I am a male survivor and former victim of relationship abuse. I was mentally hijacked, emotionally destroyed, and physically beaten by my girlfriend for almost 3 years. . . . I remember being huddled on the floor . . . as I watched, not felt, her beat me until she couldn't lift her arms anymore. . . . After a year of therapy, I still haven't found a support group for abused men.

Male offenders are often ordered to attend a Batterer's Intervention Program (BIP) as an alternative to incarceration. These group programs are typically based on methods formulated by the Duluth Domestic Abuse Intervention Project.

The Duluth approach does not ascribe to traditional counseling methodologies. Duluth interventionists do not try to develop a therapeutic relationship with the clients, even though that bond is an important predictor of psychological improvement. Nor do interventionists make a clinical diagnosis. . . .

[Male abuser] programs are "driven by ideology and stakeholder interests rather than by plausible theories and scientific evidence of cause."

Psychologist James Kline believes Duluth interventionists act as quasi-probation officers, noting that such individuals "have such narrow training and such indoctrination into the batterer model" of inter-partner violence, that it leaves them inadequate as diagnosticians and counselors.

The ideological flavor of such efforts is revealed by one program in New York State:

> The Domestic Violence Program for Men provides important, serious analysis and topics that explore the roots of sexism, racism and the other oppressions which contribute to the systemic problems leading to much of the violence men commit against their intimate partners.

The National Research Council has deplored the fact that these programs are "driven by ideology and stakeholder interests rather than by plausible theories and scientific evidence of cause."

Thus, evaluations have shown the Duluth model to have no measureable impact. Psychologist Julia Babcock once asked the rhetorical question, "Is the Duluth model set up to fail?" As researcher Donald Dutton concludes, "Research shows that Duluth-oriented treatments are absolutely ineffective, and have no discernible impact on rates of recidivism."

This review of research and policy reveals an ironic pattern of *available* services that are *in*effective, along with a general *unavailability* of services that *are* effective:

- For partners engaged in mutual violence, couples counseling is often prohibited.

- For female victims, the effectiveness of abuse shelters remains to be demonstrated.

- For female abusers, domestic violence services are generally unavailable.

- For male victims, domestic violence programs are virtually non-existent.

- For male abusers, Duluth model treatment programs are ineffective.

Restraining Orders

Restraining orders are a widely employed strategy to combat domestic violence. Sometimes known as "orders for protection," restraining orders are a legal directive that orders an individual to avoid contact and communication with his or her partner for a specified period of time.

It has been estimated that 2–3 million domestic restraining orders are issued each year in the United States. Less than half of all restraining orders involve any allegation of physical violence—the reason being that most state statutes now employ a broad definition of domestic "violence," relying on vague criteria such as "fear," "apprehension," and "emotional distress."

In theory, restraining orders appear to be a straight-foward solution to a potentially dangerous situation. The parties can be separated and the violence prevented with a minimum of legal intervention. But research and experience suggest otherwise.

Although having an order reduced psychological abuse, it was found to have no impact on threats of property damage, severe violence, or other forms of physical violence.

One early report [by P. Finn] stated, "All observers agree that—at least until they are violated—a civil protection order is useless with the 'hard core' batterer. . . . Any abuser who is determined to batter—or kill—his [or her] partner will not be deterred by a piece of paper." . . . The Independent Women's Forum has noted that restraining orders seem to only "lull women into a false sense of security."

What light does research cast on this thorny question? Four studies address this issue:

1. One early study interviewed recipients of restraining orders in Pennsylvania. Although the orders appeared to be helpful in reducing the abuse of some women with less serious histories of family violence, the authors concluded that the restraining orders were generally "ineffective in stopping physical violence."

2. A project interviewed 212 women with permanent restraining orders and compared the results of the interviews with those for 143 women not having such orders. Although having an order reduced psychological abuse, it was found to have no impact on threats of property damage, severe violence, or other forms of physical violence.

3. A third study followed 150 women in Houston, Texas, who met initial screening criteria for a permanent restraining order. Of these women, 81 were actually granted the order and 69 were not. The two groups of women were interviewed five times during an 18-month period. The women reported the same levels of threats, physical abuse, and stalking, regardless of whether they had received a restraining order or not.

4. An analysis [by L. Dugan, D. Nagin, and R. Rosenfeld] of the availability of domestic violence resources in 48 major cities and the impact of those resources on partner violence concluded, "The adoption of certain types of protection order statutes is associated with both *decreases* in black married female victimization and *increases* in the number of black women killed by their unmarried partners."

The research can be summarized as follows:

• Restraining orders may reduce psychological abuse.

• Restraining orders are generally ineffective in preventing future physical violence.

• Among unmarried partners, such orders may increase future violence.

Restraining orders are not a panacea for partner violence, and may work only for couples at low risk of abuse.

Mandatory Arrest

Mandatory arrest for partner assault has been a hotly debated topic over the past 25 years, and the focus of a number of evaluation studies as well. The first study, the Minneapolis Domestic Violence Experiment, found that arrest led to substantial reductions in subsequent violence. But the Minneapolis study was hampered by a short follow-up period and small sample size.

Follow-up studies failed to confirm the Minneapolis results. In Colorado Springs, researchers [R.A. Berk and others] concluded, "An arrest can sometimes make things worse." And in Milwaukee, arrests were found to cause an overall *increase* in partner violence among Black women, [with L.W. Sherman and others] noting that "an across-the-board policy of mandatory arrest prevents 2,504 acts of violence against primarily white women, at the price of 5,409 acts of violence against primarily Black women."

There is no evidence that prosecution of restraining order violations reduces subsequent abuse.

Furthermore, these studies did not account for the fact that mandatory arrest might discourage victims from seeking police assistance in the event of future abuse. That possibility was examined by Harvard economist Radha Iyengar, who analyzed the impact of the passage of mandatory arrest laws in 15 states. Her surprising conclusion: "Intimate partner homicides increased by about 60% in states with mandatory arrest laws."

The evidence consistently shows mandatory arrest policies cause more harm than good. Furthermore, if a state has mandatory arrest, the likelihood of subsequent conviction drops by more than half. Lawrence Sherman, director of the Milwaukee study, has termed mandatory arrest policies a "failure" and recommended that such policies be repealed.

In 33 states, violation of a restraining order is cause for mandatory arrest. Breaches of such orders appear to be common, with studies reporting violation rates ranging from 35% over a 12-month period to 44% over an 18-month period.

Violations of such orders occur for a variety of reasons. In some cases the offender continues to harass the victim. Sometimes the couple decides to re-unite but forgets to have the order rescinded.

There is no evidence that prosecution of restraining order violations reduces subsequent abuse, and one Department of Justice–funded study found that such policies place victims at greater risk. "Increases in the willingness of prosecutors' offices to take cases of protection order violation were associated with *increases in the homicide* of White married intimates, Black unmarried intimates, and White unmarried females," the study concluded.

In a well-intentioned effort to "get tough" on domestic violence, the majority of states have enacted laws that mandate arrest for alleged assault or violation of a restraining order.

Victims who summon the police usually want the situation to be stabilized; they don't want their partner to be arrested. Eventually, victims whose partners are subject to mandatory arrest are less likely to request police assistance.

Mandatory arrest laws have given rise to a range of civil rights abuses, including the undermining of probable cause, disregard of the notion of innocent-until-proven-guilty, and gender-profiling in the name of predominant aggressor assessment.

No-Drop Prosecution

The majority of abuse cases involve disputes in which the conflict is a minor, mutual, and/or one-time occurrence. The victim usually believes that these situations can be better handled through counseling or a short "cooling-off" period rather than legal intervention. So in about 80% of cases, the person who requests police assistance later recants or drops the charges.

But many jurisdictions have reached the conclusion that persons charged with abuse should be prosecuted regardless of the claimant's request. So they have instituted so-called "no-drop" policies, which require continued prosecution of the case. One survey revealed that 66% of prosecutors' offices have implemented such policies.

But no-drop policies can do a disservice to both alleged abusers and victims. They eliminate prosecutorial discretion, thus increasing the likelihood of frivolous legal action. If the defendant is poor, he or she will have to rely on the counsel of an already over-burdened public defender. In many cases, the accused accepts a plea bargain arrangement that requires admitting to having committed a lesser crime, even if no violence had occurred.

Victims want their voices to be heard, not silenced.

If the alleged victim refuses to testify, the prosecutor may charge obstruction of justice and threaten to take away the children. In one California case, a county prosecutor put a woman in jail for 8 days after she refused to testify against her boyfriend. She later won a $125,000 settlement for false imprisonment.

Aggressive prosecution policies dissuade women from seeking future police assistance, as well. One survey of female victims in Quincy, Mass. found that among women who did not report a subsequent incident of abuse, 56% believed that the victim has no say or rights in the criminal justice system. In contrast, among women who did report such incidents, only 12% shared that belief.

Echoing these findings, law professor Kimberle Crenshaw has argued that "many women of color are reluctant to seek intervention from the police, fearing that contact with law enforcement will exacerbate the system's assault on their public and personal lives." As the Ms. Foundation for Women notes, victims want their voices to be heard, not silenced.

Only one randomized study has evaluated the effectiveness of varying levels of prosecution on subsequent aggression. The research found that only one factor reduced abuser recidivism—allowing the victim to select whether and how aggressively the prosecutor would pursue the case. Obviously a no-drop prosecution policy eliminates the opportunity for the victim to make that choice.

One analysis [by R.C. Davis, B.E. Smith, and H.J. Davies] reached this sobering conclusion: "We do not know whether no-drop increases victim safety or places the victims in greater jeopardy."

The Violence Against Women Act authorizes $225 million for STOP (Services, Training, Officers, and Prosecutors) grants, of which at least 25%—about $56 million—is allocated to prosecutorial activities. In two-thirds of jurisdictions, prosecutors are bound by domestic violence no-drop policies.

But we do not know whether such policies are helpful, harmful, or have no effect at all.

Symbolism over Substance

Declines in intimate partner homicides began in the mid-1970s, and trend lines continued on the same course following passage of the Family Violence Prevention and Services Act in 1984 and the Violence Against Women Act in 1994.

This report examined the evidence supporting the effectiveness of four widely used violence-reduction strategies: abuser treatment, restraining orders, mandatory arrest, and no-drop prosecution. This review reveals that:

- Abuser treatment services are either ineffective, or those known to be effective are generally unavailable.

- Restraining orders generally have no impact on subsequent physical abuse.

- Mandatory arrest laws substantially increase homicides, discourage future requests for police assistance, and reduce conviction rates.

- We do not know whether no-drop prosecution increases, reduces, or has no impact on future violence.

In sum, we conclude that domestic violence programs are generally ineffective and sometimes harmful. Others have reached a similar conclusion:

- Leading family violence researcher Richard Gelles stated, "Policy and practice based on these factoids and theory might actually be harmful to women, men, children, and the institution of the family."

- New York University vice provost Linda Mills concluded: "At worst, the criminal justice system increases violence against women. At best, it has little or no effect."

- Researcher John Hamel wrote, "Current policy toward domestic violence, including criminal justice and mental health responses . . . has proven to be shortsighted and limited in its effectiveness."

So why have these policies been allowed to persist?

University of Hawaii law professor Virginia Hench has noted that these policies are "a classic example of a 'get tough' policy that has symbolic value with the electorate, but which can lead to a host of problems." Hench concludes that if we "choose symbols over substance, that is a true failure to support those victims" of violence.

CHAPTER 4

What Are the Consequences of Family Violence?

Chapter Preface

Intimate partner violence (IPV) and child abuse—the two most prevalent forms of family violence—inflict severe consequences on the victim and impose significant costs on society. A 2007 Centers for Disease Control and Prevention (CDC) study placed the annual cost of intimate partner violence to US society at $8.9 billion, including the direct costs of medical and mental health care and the indirect costs of lost productivity. The CDC estimated that victims of severe intimate partner violence lose nearly 8 million days of paid work, the equivalent of thirty-two thousand full-time jobs.

IPV also leads to higher health-care costs for employers. According to a 2010 study by the Robert Wood Johnson Foundation, the direct cost of IPV to businesses is nearly $6 billion per year, including $4 billion for health-care services. The indirect impact of lost productivity costs businesses an additional $728 million a year, the foundation reported.

Child abuse and neglect are even more costly to society. The study conducted by Xiangming Fang and associates titled "The Economic Burden of Child Maltreatment in the United States and Implications for Prevention," which appeared in the February 2012 issue of the journal *Child Abuse & Neglect*, reported:

> The estimated average lifetime cost per victim of nonfatal child maltreatment is $210,012 in 2010 dollars, including $32,648 in childhood health care costs; $10,530 in adult medical costs; $144,360 in productivity losses; $7,728 in child welfare costs; $6,747 in criminal justice costs; and $7,999 in special education costs. The estimated average lifetime cost per death is $1,272,900, including $14,100 in medical costs and $1,258,800 in productivity losses. The total lifetime economic burden resulting from new cases of fatal

and nonfatal child maltreatment in the United States in 2008 is approximately $124 billion.

The personal consequences to the victim of intimate partner abuse can be catastrophic both physically and psychologically. In 2005, according to the CDC, 329 males and 1,181 females were murdered by an intimate partner. In 2008, females aged twelve or older experienced about 552,000 nonfatal violent victimizations, including rape/sexual assault, robbery, and aggravated or simple assault by an intimate partner, according to the Bureau of Justice Statistics. In the same year, males experienced 101,000 nonfatal violent victimizations by an intimate partner.

The long-term impact on a victim's health can be as devastating as the physical injury sustained during the attack. According to the 2010 National Intimate Partner and Sexual Violence Survey conducted by the CDC:

> Men and women who experienced rape or stalking by any perpetrator or physical violence by an intimate partner in their lifetime were more likely to report frequent headaches, chronic pain, difficulty with sleeping, activity limitations, poor physical health, and poor mental health than men and women who did not experience these forms of violence. Women who had experienced these forms of violence were also more likely to report having asthma, irritable bowel syndrome, and diabetes than women who did not experience these forms of violence.

Child abuse is equally damaging to the victim. The CDC has concluded that childhood abuse and neglect lead to a multitude of health and social problems. These problems include alcoholism, depression, illicit drug use, liver disease, risk for intimate partner violence, early initiation of sexual activity and multiple sex partners, sexually transmitted diseases, smoking, suicide attempts, and unintended pregnancies.

In the following chapter, different perspectives are presented on the consequences of family violence.

Girls Exposed to Intimate Partner Violence Are at Increased Risk for Alcohol Abuse in Adulthood

Laura J. Elwyn, Timothy O. Ireland, Carolyn A. Smith, and Terence P. Thornberry.

Laura J. Elwyn and Carolyn A. Smith are with the School of Social Welfare, State University of New York at Albany; Timothy O. Ireland is with the Department of Criminology and Criminal Justice, Niagara University; and Terence P. Thornberry is with the Department of Criminology and Criminal Justice, University of Maryland.

Substance use has been and remains a significant public health target associated with multiple disruptions in family life and substantial personal and societal costs, including heightened risk for intimate partner violence. Violence in the family is also a national public health concern in view of its frequency, its immediate health and safety concerns for victims, and its short- and long-term effects across a range of developmental domains.

Research into the consequences of family violence has historically been grouped into two fairly distinct sets of literatures. One line of inquiry examines the consequences of directly experienced childhood or adolescent maltreatment. Recent prospective research establishes that maltreatment is a relatively robust predictor of delinquency, crime, conduct problems, and possibly long-term drug and alcohol use among

Laura J. Elwyn, Timothy O. Ireland, Carolyn A. Smith, Terence P. Thornberry, "Impact of Adolescent Exposure to Intimate Partner Violence on Substance Abuse in Early Adulthood," *Journal of Studies on Alcohol and Drugs*, v. 71, no. 2, March 2010, p. 219. Copyright 2010. Reproduced by permission of ALCOHOL RESEARCH DOCUMENTATION, INC. in the format Textbook/Other book via Copyright Clearance Center.

women. The second line of research considers the consequences of experiencing family violence vicariously by either witnessing IPV [intimate partner violence] or living in a home rife with serious conflict. However, the developmental consequences of growing up in a partner-violent family are less understood than the consequences of maltreatment. In fact, very few longitudinal [long-term] studies of links between exposure to parental IPV and substance use among young adults exist. . . . Furthermore, because each line of research explores a narrow category of family violence, the specific impact of one type of family violence net of other types of family violence remains an open question.

Approximately 15.5 million American children live in dual-parent households in which partner-violence has occurred in the past year.

Although the intertwined relationship between family violence and substance use can be illuminated in a variety of ways, the facet explored here focuses on adolescent exposure to parental (or guardian) IPV and subsequent substance-use patterns in young adulthood. . . .

Assessing the prevalence of child exposure to parental partner violence is complicated because there is little uniformity in definitions of IPV. In addition, whether a child living in the home actually witnesses IPV remains largely unknown. As a result, the estimate of the number of children exposed to IPV remains very incomplete. Generally, community surveys find that about one in six couples experience IPV annually. Rates are higher among younger couples, cohabiting couples, and couples with children. [R.J.] McDonald [and colleagues] estimated that "approximately 15.5 million American children live in dual-parent households in which partner-violence has occurred in the past year." Others have estimated that between 10% and 20% of children, or up to 10 million children annually, are exposed to IPV . . . and . . . that about four of five children living in a partner-violent home witness or hear partner violence.

In contrast, a number of national studies monitor substance use and abuse during adolescence and young adulthood. For example, using *Monitoring the Future*, [L.D.] Johnston [and colleagues] estimated that in 2006, 73% of 12th graders used alcohol, and 56% reported "being drunk," and these prevalence rates increased in young adulthood to 89% and 81%, respectively. Use of illegal substances, from marijuana to heroin and crack, is also quite common, with 50% of 12th graders and graduating seniors using some illegal drug, most commonly marijuana. In young adulthood, the proportion rises to about 60%, with drug use other than marijuana at 35%. About 10% of adults go on to develop a drug-use disorder during their lives. . . .

Few Studies Exist

Although a range of behavioral problems are noted among children raised in partner-violent homes, the most frequently observed problems are aggression and antisocial behavior. The most frequently noted problems among adults retrospectively reporting childhood exposure to IPV include antisocial behavior, as well as partner violence, although other problems, including depression, posttraumatic stress disorder, and alcohol and drug abuse, are also noted. Recent reviews and meta-analyses of exposure to IPV studies also conclude that a wide range of outcomes across multiple domains and across a variety of developmental periods (i.e., childhood, adolescence, and adulthood) may be affected by IPV exposure. No reviews, however, identify substance-use problems as a consequence of exposure to IPV. . . .

Whether exposure to IPV is a risk factor for subsequent substance abuse remains an open question. We could find no truly prospective studies that consider the potential impact of victim characteristics such as gender, characteristics of the abuse such as its severity, and characteristics of the parents, including their substance-use history. Often the unique role of exposure to IPV is unclear because of the measured or unmeasured impact of other forms of family violence and other adversities. . . .

Despite theoretical indications that exposure to IPV should have significant life-course consequences, there are substantial gaps in our existing knowledge base as it pertains to subsequent substance use. Overall, we address the general hypothesis that exposure to IPV during adolescence predicts young adult substance-use problems. The following research questions are addressed: (a) Is adolescent exposure to IPV associated with substance-use problems in early adulthood net of other factors including child maltreatment and parental substance use? (b) Does the relationship between exposure to adolescent IPV and early adult substance-use problems differ by gender?

Urban Youth Were Studied

Data for this study were drawn from the RYDS [Rochester Youth Development Study], which was designed to investigate the development of delinquency and other problem behaviors in a representative urban community sample. . . . The RYDS is a multiwave panel study in which youths and their primary caretakers, generally the mother, were initially interviewed every 6 months, and then at three annual interviews in young adulthood. Data were collected in two phases. During the first phase, participants were, on average, 14–18 years old; during the second phase they were 21–23 years old. Measures used here were gathered from youth and parental interviews in Phases 1 and 2 or collected from official agencies. All human subject protections were observed and the study has been continually monitored by the institutional review board of the University at Albany.

The initial sample of 1,000 adolescents was selected from the population of seventh and eighth graders in the Rochester, NY, public schools in 1987. Given the original interest in serious delinquency, high-risk youth were oversampled on sex (75% males, 25% females) and on residence in high-crime areas of the city. . . . The original panel included 68% African American, 17% Latino, and 15% White participants. A range of field procedures has been successfully used throughout the study to minimize attrition over time. At the end of the second phase of data collection, in early adulthood, 85% (846) of the initial 1,000 [youth] participants were reinterviewed. A comparison of those retained and not retained at the end of Phase 2 revealed no significant differences in demographic characteristics and delinquency between the original panel and those retained. . . .

The association between exposure to severe IPV in adolescence and alcohol-use problems in early adulthood does indeed differ by sex.

The predicted odds of alcohol-use problems for young men exposed to severe IPV in adolescence were almost the same as the predicted odds for young men not exposed to severe IPV, controlling for other factors. . . . Young women exposed to severe IPV, however, had significantly higher predicted odds of alcohol-use problems than young women not exposed to severe IPV. . . .

We found that exposure to IPV—either total or severe—in adolescence does not predict drug- or alcohol-use problems in early adulthood for males, who comprised the majority of our sample. However, we did find one significant difference between males and females in the relationship between exposure to IPV and AOD [alcohol and other drug] outcomes. Our findings indicate that, for this urban sample, the association between exposure to severe IPV in adolescence and alcohol-use problems in early adulthood does indeed differ by sex. . . .

The study adds new knowledge to the family-violence and substance-abuse fields. Overall, but particularly for the young men in this high-risk community sample, we found less association between adolescent exposure to IPV and early adult substance-use problems than we expected. For young women, however, we found a positive relationship between exposure to IPV in adolescence and alcohol problems in early adulthood. This is consistent with evidence of a stronger relationship between child maltreatment and adult alcohol problems for women, and indicates the need for efforts targeted at preventing adverse outcomes resulting from family violence for young women.

Women Experiencing Family Violence Are More Likely to Suffer from Postpartum Depression

Susan London

Susan London is a writer for Clinical Psychiatry News.

Abuse is prevalent in the period surrounding pregnancy and is associated with a higher rate of postpartum depression, but certain factors might help identify abused women who are at highest risk and might benefit from targeted screening and intervention.

In a national survey of Canadian women who recently had given birth, 11% reported abuse in the past 2 years, according to study results. . . .

Abused women were roughly three times more likely than their nonabused counterparts to have postpartum depression. Within the abused group, the risk of postpartum depression was more than doubled for teenagers and women aged 35 years or older, as well as for women who were depressed before pregnancy.

Prevalence of Abuse

Several studies in the past few decades have explored the issue of violence around the time of pregnancy. "Yet, despite that, we actually don't have good estimates of prevalence" for reasons that include variation in the types of abuse captured, the time period and perpetrators assessed, and the women studied, noted Patricia J. O'Campo, Ph.D.

Susan London, "Family Violence Predicts Postpartum Depression," *Clinical Psychiatry News*, v. 39, no. 2, February 2011, p. 23. All rights reserved. Reproduced by permission.

In the national population-based study—the Maternity Experiences Survey—Dr. O'Campo and her colleagues used census data to identify Canadian women with a singleton infant aged 5–14 months.

Abused women most often indicated that they had been pushed, grabbed, or shoved; were threatened with being hit; or had something thrown at them.

A random sample was selected for a computer-assisted telephone interview that asked whether they had experienced any of 10 types of abuse (actual or threatened) in the past 2 years, as well as questions from the EPDS (Edinburgh Postnatal Depression Scale).

Interviews were conducted with 6,421 women, who represented a weighted sample of 76,508 women, according to Dr. O'Campo, an epidemiologist at the University of Toronto. Most were 5–9 months post partum (average, 7.3 months).

Fully 11% of the women reported experiencing abuse in the past 2 years. In stratified analyses, the prevalence was highest among teenagers (40%); women having an annual income of less than $20,000 (28%); aboriginal women (30%); and nonmarried, noncohabiting women (35%).

By far, the leading perpetrators were partners (reported by 6% overall), followed by family members (2%), strangers/others (2%), and friends (1%).

Abused women most often indicated that they had been pushed, grabbed, or shoved; were threatened with being hit; or had something thrown at them, according to Dr. O'Campo. And they most commonly reported that just one incident of abuse had occurred, and that the abuse had taken place only before pregnancy.

The patterns regarding the type and timing of abuse and the perpetrator overall were generally the same among low-income and nonmarried subgroups, but those two subgroups differed with respect to the frequency of abuse, more commonly reporting two to five incidents or six or more.

"The 11%, I think, is significant," she commented, noting that previous population-based studies have found prevalences of less than 5% for 1-year periods. "But I think it could be higher, actually, if we had had a full spectrum of abuse items that were asked about," she added.

The diverse nature of perpetrators suggests that future research should not focus solely on partners, according to Dr. O'Campo. "Contrary to common perception," abuse is not necessarily a high risk around the time of pregnancy; "in fact, it's lower than, say, the abuse that was experienced before pregnancy," she further observed.

Predictors of Postpartum Depression

"Exposure to family violence is increasingly understood to be an important risk factor for adverse pregnancy outcomes," said coinvestigator Patricia A. Janssen, Ph.D. "But its role in the development of postpartum depression has not been well studied yet."

Certain psychosocial factors have been linked to the risk of family violence and postpartum depression, questioning the relationship between the two, she added.

Overall, 8% of the women in the survey screened positive for postpartum depression (defined as a score of at least 13 of 30 on the EPDS), reported Dr. Janssen, an epidemiologist at the University of British Columbia in Vancouver.

The rate was nearly threefold higher among abused women (17%) than among their nonabused counterparts (6%). Within the abused group, the risk of postpartum depression was more than doubled for women who were younger than age 20 or aged 35 years or older relative to their peers aged 20–34 years. In addition, the risk was more than twice as high for abused women who had depression before pregnancy. Marital status, education, employment, ethnicity and immigration status, income, and whether pregnancy was planned did not significantly influence this outcome among abused women.

In adjusted analyses that focused on the timing of abuse, women who were abused only before pregnancy, starting after pregnancy, or before, during, and after pregnancy were all significantly more likely to have postpartum depression than were their nonabused peers. The results were generally the same when women with preexisting depression were excluded.

When analyses were restricted to just the threatened types of abuse, risk was significantly elevated among women whose abuse occurred only before pregnancy, began during pregnancy and continued afterward, started after pregnancy, or occurred before, during, and after pregnancy. Again, the results were generally the same when women with preexisting depression were excluded.

"Women who are abused have higher rates of postpartum depression," Dr. Janssen said. "I hope this will encourage people to screen more for abuse, if they recognize that it's a risk factor for depression."

Those at the extremes of childbearing age or with preexisting depression appear to be especially vulnerable. Thus, "if we do know that women are abused, we should be paying particular attention to the risk for postpartum depression among those women."

Victims of Domestic Violence Have Higher Health Costs

Women's Health Weekly

Women's Health Weekly *is a magazine devoted to women's health issues.*

Victims of domestic violence endure significantly higher health costs than other women for three years after the abuse ends, a [2010] study finds.

Abuse victims had health care costs that averaged more than $1,200 above non-abused women for the first two years after the abuse ended and about $400 above others in the third year.

"Women may continue to experience physical and emotional consequences even years after their abuse ends, and that is reflected in their health care costs," said Amy Bonomi, co-author of the study and associate professor of human development and family science at Ohio State University.

The study was led by Paul Fishman of the Group Health Research Institute in Seattle. . . .

The study is the first to look at how health care costs of abused women change from year to year after abuse ends. This study looked at costs during the years of abuse and then during each year up to 10 years later.

The results suggest that domestic abuse acts on health care costs much like chronic health conditions, Bonomi said.

"The prolonged impact of abuse on health care costs is consistent with what we find with people who quit smoking or abusing alcohol or drugs—the costs don't go back to normal for years," she said.

The study involved 2,026 women patients at Group Health Cooperative, a health system in the Pacific Northwest. All women in the study consented to giving researchers confidential access to their medical records.

Abused women's health care costs were $585 greater per year than non-abused women during the period of abuse.

Women in the study were surveyed by telephone about whether they experienced any physical, sexual or psychological abuse from intimate partners, including husbands and boyfriends, since they were 18 years old. Women who indicated any abuse were asked which year each abuse type started and stopped.

In all, 859 women reported some type of abuse in their adult lifetime and 1,167 reported no abuse.

The researchers then looked at the women's health care costs through Group Health from 1992 through 2002, In order to make sure that it was the abuse that was driving the cost differences between abused and non-abused women, the study took into account a wide variety of factors that may also be related, including the women's age, race and ethnicity, education and income, marital and employment status, among other influences.

Of those who reported abuse, about one-quarter said their abuse was "extremely severe," while about 39 percent said their abuse was "not severe" or "slightly severe."

Overall, abused women's health care costs were $585 greater per year than non-abused women during the period of abuse. After the abuse ended, health costs were $1,231 higher in the first year, $1,204 higher the second year, and $444 higher the third year. By the fourth year after abuse, health care costs were similar to that of other women.

Bonomi said the researchers don't have data to explain why health care costs are actually higher for the first two years after abuse ends than they were during the years of abuse. However, she believes she has one possible explanation.

"Women may not be accessing health care services that they should be while they are with an abusive partner. They may fear retaliation, particularly if they are in a controlling relationship."

In addition, women may be more likely to seek mental health services to help them cope once they are free from the abusive relationship.

If anything, Bonomi said the study may underestimate the extra health care costs borne by victims of domestic abuse. Some victims participating in the study may not have admitted to being abused, so were not included among the abuse victims.

Also, the study counts all types of abuse the same—from severe physical and sexual abuse to controlling behavior that could qualify as psychological abuse.

"Our findings are conservative; it is likely that the true health care costs for many abused women are higher than what we report," Bonomi said.

Bonomi said the results show that abuse prevention efforts can actually save the health care industry significant amounts of money.

"Victims of abuse require more health care resources for years after their abuse ends. If we can prevent domestic violence, we are not only helping the women involved, we are also saving money in our health care system."

Intimate Partner Violence Has a Negative Impact on the Workplace

Carole A. Reeves and Anne M. O'Leary-Kelly

Carole A. Reeves is vice-provost for entrepreneurship at the University of Arkansas, and Anne M. O'Leary-Kelly is a professor of management at the University of Arkansas.

A number of previous studies suggest that women who experience intimate partner violence (IPV) carry the effects with them to work. In small scale studies and anecdotal reports, victimized women have reported that the abuse caused them to be absent and tardy, to be less productive while at work, to lose advancement opportunities, to lose their jobs, and to earn lower wages. In spite of this evidence and research showing that IPV has been experienced by a significant percentage of Americans, most employers have done little to address the issue.

The purpose of this research was to better understand how IPV affects the workplace. If the effects are negligible, this suggests that managers are wise to limit the attention given to the IPV phenomenon; if the effects are negative and significant, this suggests that prudent employers will give greater attention to IPV as an organizational issue. We examined the impact of IPV on the workplace in two distinct phases. In the first phase, we focused on two research questions:

1. Does IPV affect employees, and, if so, how?

2. What is the impact of IPV on organizations?

In the second phase of the research, we examined the ways that IPV plays out within the organizational environment, with a particular emphasis on coworker-related actions and effects. Specifically, we examined the following research questions:

1. Does work-related social support have positive effects on the well-being, attitudes, and behaviors of employed IPV victims?

2. How and when will coworkers provide assistance to IPV victims at work?

3. When and to whom will IPV victims disclose their victimization at work?

4. What organizational conditions are associated with stronger feelings of hopefulness on the part of employed IPV victims?

The sample for the first phase of the study was composed of 1,588 women and 838 men who worked in three midsized business organizations headquartered in a southern state. The sample for the second phase was composed of 2,063 women and 688 men who worked in a midsized financial services institution headquartered in the same state. In both phases of the study, respondents completed a web-based survey with questions regarding general work-life questions. . . .

How Does IPV Affect Employees?

Research Question One: Does IPV affect employees, and, if so, how? We found high rates of IPV among employed individuals in both phases of the study. In Phase One, 10.3% of women and 10.4% of men reported abuse within the past 12 months (these individuals were labeled "current victims"). Furthermore, an additional 30% of women and 19.2% of men reported experiencing IPV sometime in their lifetimes (other than the past 12 months; these individuals were labeled "lifetime victims"). In Phase Two, 8% of women and 8.4% of men reported abuse within the past 12 months, and an additional 27.3% of women and 12.1% of men reported lifetime IPV.

The most prevalent form of abuse at work was stalking.

At first glance it appears that total current victimization rates were the same for men and women in our study. However, while we found no significant difference in rates of total current victimization, we found striking differences in the types of violence experienced by male and female employees. Female employees who were experiencing current victimization were more likely than current male victims to experience four of the five types of violence (threatening, stalking, being hurt, and sexual violence). The exception was physical aggression (hitting, slapping, kicking, punching, scratching, pushing, biting or other use of physical force), which was more likely to have been experienced by current male than current female victims. However, when looking at *degree* of victimization, we found that females who experienced physical aggression experienced it much more frequently than males. Overall, then, while there were similar percentages of male and female employees reporting some level of IPV victimization, female employees reported more frequent and more severe IPV. This is consistent with previous research that found higher rates of injury and medical usage for women than men.

Our findings also demonstrate that a large number of IPV incidents occur at work. Over 20% of the employees who reported that they currently were being victimized indicated that some form of IPV had occurred on their work premises. The most prevalent form of abuse at work was stalking; of those victims who had experienced stalking, over 51% indicated that it had occurred at least once on work premises. Threats of physical harm were also fairly frequent, with over 7% of those who experienced this form of IPV indicating that it had occurred at least once on work premises. These numbers suggest that many workplaces are directly affected by IPV.

To better understand how IPV affects employed individuals, we analyzed personal and professional well-being data from the Phase One sample. Our results indicate that IPV is negatively associated with personal well-being for both current and lifetime victims. Essentially, we found that both male and female victimized employees experience higher levels of depression and lower levels of self-esteem and economic self-sufficiency than their non-victimized colleagues. Because previous research establishes the importance of a woman's income to her likelihood of abuse, it seems probable that confidence in one's own economic power will be critical to the ability of a victimized woman to extricate herself from a dysfunctional family situation. Although our study reiterates well-established findings regarding the negative effects of IPV on personal well-being, it is worth noting again that our sample included only working people. It could be argued that employed victims are among the most "well-functioning" of victims in that they are interacting in the world and maintaining a job. It is noteworthy, then, that IPV takes a significant toll on personal well-being even with these individuals.

Professional Well-Being

We also found negative effects of IPV on professional well-being, but the results were less universal. Not surprisingly, currently victimized employees reported more difficulty in integrating their family and work demands, but this difficulty was not reported by lifetime victims. There was no correlation between current victimization and the two other professional well-being variables we examined—self-efficacy and job insecurity. Thus, there is no evidence that current victims feel less capable of performing their jobs or feel less confident concerning the security of their jobs. On the other hand, there was no relationship between lifetime victimization and family-work conflict or self-efficacy, but there was a positive relation-ship between lifetime victimization and job insecurity. Con-necting our results on personal well-being with those on professional well-being, perhaps the negative effects of IPV on factors such as depression and self-esteem have long-term ef-fects on victims' sense of security in holding their jobs. In summary, the findings from our large-scale study provide strong evidence in support of previous anecdotal reports and small-scale studies—IPV is experienced by large numbers of employed individuals and it negatively affects them.

Our study also revealed an effect of victimization on work distraction, with current victims reporting signifi-cantly higher levels of distraction compared to non-victims.

Research Question Two: What is the impact of IPV on orga-nizations? Our research suggests that IPV victimization has negative effects on employee work outcomes and that these ef-fects have costs for employers in terms of absenteeism and work distraction. Although we note that caution must be taken in generalizing the findings beyond the companies in-volved in this research, the results of this study add to a grow-ing body of evidence suggesting that the effects of family vio-lence are pervasive, with negative effects extending beyond the victims and their families.

First, our findings indicate that victimization affects work absence. Specifically, we found that employees who are life-time IPV victims were more likely to be tardy and absent than were non-victims. It was interesting, however, that employees who currently were experiencing IPV were no more likely to be absent than were non-victims. Our study also revealed an effect of victimization on work distraction, with current vic-tims reporting significantly higher levels of distraction com-pared to non-victims. This effect indicates that employees who currently are experiencing IPV have more difficulty staying engaged in their work than do non-victims, a finding that is not surprising given the trauma of IPV. But it is noteworthy that we found no differences in the levels of work distraction for lifetime victims vs. non-victimized employees.

These findings suggest an interesting pattern of effects depending upon the recency of victimization. Simply put, it appears that current victims get to work, but have more difficulty working than non-victims, and this pattern was especially strong for female victims. On the other hand, lifetime victims appear to have challenges around work attendance, but once at work, they are as fully engaged as other employees. Taken together, these findings suggest that victimization has short and long-term detrimental effects on work-related outcomes, but also that IPV victims can recover, particularly in terms of their work productivity. . . .

Work-Related Social Support

Research Question Three: Does work-related social support have positive effects on the well-being, attitudes, and behaviors of employed IPV victims? We examined how social support from co-workers and the organization affected the well-being of employed IPV victims. Although it seems reasonable to expect that victims who have support would be better off than those who did not, it also is possible that IPV victims are in such a difficult life state that support from people at work is not influential to their well-being. Our results suggest that support from the organization, not from coworkers, is most influential in predicting well-being variables. IPV victims who felt supported by their organization (compared to those who did not) reported less depression, higher job satisfaction, stronger organizational commitment, less job insecurity, and a lower intention to leave the job situation. However, the positive effects of organizational support did not extend to behavioral outcomes; that is, perceptions of organizational support were not associated with absenteeism or work distraction levels of IPV victims. Contrary to our expectations, support from coworkers did little to impact the well-being of victims in either a positive or negative direction. The only exception to this was that coworker support was associated with higher job satisfaction and with less job insecurity. Taken together, these results suggest that it is the support of the employer that is most critical to the overall well-being of IPV victims.

Do Coworkers Help Victims?

Research Question Four: How and when will coworkers provide assistance to IPV victims at work? Twenty percent (470) of employees (excluding current victims, who did not answer questions about coworkers' victimization) reported knowing about a colleague who worked in their current organization who had been victimized by IPV. Of these coworkers, 408 (87%) indicated that they had provided some type of support to their victimized colleague. Although a high percentage of coworkers indicated that they had provided some type of support, the degree of assistance provided to IPV victims was relatively low. Coworkers most often provided assistance in the form of giving advice about the relationship or about assistance services available to IPV victims. The most common action other than advice-giving was sharing information with others in the workplace (e.g., supervisor, HR [human resources] professional, security professional).

We also examined factors that predicted coworker assistance. Interestingly, neither coworker personality factors, nor the coworker's attachment to the organization, nor the degree of negative effect of the IPV on the coworker were predictive of assistance-giving. However, the coworker's gender, similarity to the victim, and the coworker's source of knowledge about victimization (e.g., learning through personal experiences such as being directly told or witnessing an incident rather than passive learning like hearing from a third party) were associated with assistance-giving.

These findings suggest a complex picture of coworker involvement with victims. Coworkers appeared to limit their level of assistance, and to provide assistance primarily when they felt compelled to because of a direct experience or a perceived connection (e.g., to help out other women). However, coworkers were not unsympathetic to victims, in that a strong majority who knew about a colleague's victimization provided some form of assistance. Perhaps it is fair to say that coworkers, at least in the organization we studied, might be regarded as "sympathetic but reluctant observers" to the IPV victimization.

The pattern of disclosure we uncovered . . . tended to be with supervisors and coworkers rather than with more distant and formal organizational authorities.

Research Question Five: When and to whom will IPV victims disclose their victimization at work? We asked individuals who self-identified as current victims to indicate their level of disclosure to four disclosure targets: the supervisor, coworkers, an HR professional in the organization, or a security professional in the organization. Overall, 124 of 224 current IPV victims (55%) indicated that they had disclosed their victimization to someone at work; however, the level of disclosure by IPV victims was quite low (in terms of the degree of information shared). The pattern of disclosure we uncovered was interesting. When disclosure did occur, it tended to be with supervisors and coworkers rather than with more distant and formal organizational authorities, such as HR representatives or security personnel. In effect, we found that IPV victims disclose their victimization to individuals who are close in their social work space.

We asked current IPV victims who reported they had disclosed their victimization to someone at work about their motives for disclosure. These motives were categorized into those that primarily served the victim's needs (e.g., time off, emotional support, protection) and those that primarily served organizational/coworker needs (e.g., affecting coworkers, worrying about coworkers' safety). We found that disclosure was most likely to occur when victims needed something or wanted to explain their poor job performance or attendance. These results lead us to two conclusions. First, the workplace *does* serve as a source of needed information and resources for IPV victims. Second, victims' need for these organization-based resources is powerful. If victims are willing to overcome their reluctance to disclose their abuse, then the needs that prompt this disclosure must be strong indeed.

We also found that when IPV victims disclosed to someone at work, the effects were more positive than negative. Certainly, disclosure has the potential to make the victim a social isolate or to lead others to develop less positive perceptions of the victim. In our sample, victims who had disclosed did not report these effects. On the contrary, they reported feeling more hopeful, safer, more supported, and better able to concentrate.

How Can Victims Become More Hopeful?

Research Question Six: What organizational conditions are associated with stronger feelings of hopefulness on the part of employed IPV victims? In order to understand what might make IPV victims feel more hopeful about their life situation, we examined the association between hopefulness and multiple other constructs. We found a positive relationship between the amount of support that IPV victims receive from their organization and their level of hopefulness. We also found a positive relationship between victims' economic self-sufficiency and their level of hopefulness and a negative relationship between job insecurity and hopefulness. Taken together, these results demonstrate the critical role of economic empowerment for IPV victims. Given that hope is a goal-oriented mental state, victims who are hopeful are more likely to take action to change their life situation. Our findings, therefore, demonstrate a strong connection between economic empowerment and the hopeful mental state that is needed for victims to break the cycle of violence that entraps them.

When we examined the extent to which victims' hopefulness about the future was associated with various professional and personal variables, we found a positive association between hopefulness and organizational commitment and job satisfaction and a negative association between hopefulness and depression, work distraction, and intention to turnover. There was not, however, a significant relationship between hopefulness and absenteeism.

Hope Is Important

We believe our finding that IPV victims who disclose their abuse at work are more hopeful about their futures is critically important. In our study, hopefulness was a very important state of mind for victims. When IPV victims were hopeful about their futures, their personal and professional well-being were stronger. This suggests that hope is a powerful coping mechanism for individuals who are in the midst of IPV victimization. Victims who were able to sustain hope that their future would be better were able to function at a higher level at work, to feel more pleasure in their work, to make positive attachments to the employer, and to maintain a more positive affective state.

Older Abused Women Suffer Long-Term Psychological and Physical Effects

Julie McGarry

Julie McGarry is a program director at the School of Nursing, Midwifery, and Physiotherapy at the University of Nottingham in the United Kingdom.

Domestic abuse is a complex and largely hidden phenomenon. It encompasses a wide range of harms to people who are or have been intimate partners, including physical, emotional, sexual and financial abuse.

The consequences of domestic abuse are far-reaching, and have a significant effect on the long-term health and emotional wellbeing of those affected. However, while the existing literature offers an insight into the scope and nature of domestic abuse among the younger population, there are little available data about older women and domestic abuse. This is increasingly being recognised as a significant deficit in awareness and understanding in a societal context and more particularly for those responsible for support and care provision.

Historically a number of cultural and social factors have led to older women 'suffering in silence.' One contributory factor may be that in the UK [United Kingdom], domestic abuse has only been viewed as a crime in recent years. Indeed, many surveys and studies have excluded women over the age of 59 years, further reinforcing the view that domestic abuse only affects younger women and thereby effectively excluding and ignoring the particular experiences of older women.

Julie McGarry, "How Domestic Abuse Affects the Well-Being of Older Women: Julie McGarry and Colleagues Carried Out a Study That Looked at Why Women Have Tended to 'Suffer in Silence' at the Hands of Violent Partners," *Nursing Older People*, v. 22, no. 5, June 2010, p. 33. All rights reserved. Reproduced by permission.

From a care provision perspective, women's refuges and other domestic abuse services may not be appropriate for older women for a number of reasons; for example, lack of facilities for those with a disability and mobility issues, and an absence of the specialised support that older women may need.

While research in this area may be scarce, the work that has been undertaken to date suggests that domestic abuse is a significant and under-recognised phenomenon that has a wide-ranging effect on the lives of older women. It also suggests that older women's experiences of domestic abuse are markedly different from those in younger age groups and that these differences have not been adequately acknowledged or accounted for.

The aim of this study was to explore older women's experience of domestic abuse and its effect on their health and lives. For the purposes of this study, older women were defined as those aged 59 years and over, in recognition of the deficit of inclusion of women over the age of 59 years in previous studies of domestic abuse. . . .

The findings have been organised into the main three themes that emerged from the data:

- Stripped of identity: the effect of domestic abuse on the lives and health of older women.

- Giving permission: potential barriers to reporting abuse.

- The information vacuum: service provision for older women.

Stripped of Identity

The effect of domestic abuse has been well documented in the literature and has the potential to significantly affect women's short- and long-term physical and psychological health status. In the present study the long-term consequences of physical abuse on health in later life were identified as a particular issue for a number of participants.

'He was extremely abusive and he put me into the hospital quite a few times. The consequences on my health now . . . I have had major bone problems, and I had to have an operation on my spine, and I am questioning whether that was to do with the beatings. I've got arthritis and I had lots of broken bones when he was doing this, so whether that affected . . . I am sure that this possibly did affect me now . . . Like, now, I can hardly walk, and I have to go in a wheelchair to go about' (participant one, 63 years).

Women who have experienced domestic abuse are also at increased risk of experiencing mental health problems.

'I am waiting for a hearing aid now . . . I got severely bashed on my ear, and I am told that I can't hear at all in this ear, and I have been told that it is a perforated eardrum' (participant eight, 76 years).

Women who have experienced domestic abuse are also at increased risk of experiencing mental health problems such as depression. Many of those in the present study had experienced a number of psychological problems, at the time of the abuse and also in later life; for example, panic attacks and acute anxiety.

'In enduring this period of abuse I have had lots and lots of mental health problems. I have been in and out of the hospital having violent attacks of acute anxiety, they said, that is what they call them . . . they said it was acute anxiety, because I didn't have the tools to manage what he was doing to me' (participant one, 63 years).

'The long-term impact on my health has been depression . . . I had it then when all that was going on and now for ten years . . . nearly 12 years' (participant seven, 75 years).

'Because I don't want to be out more than two or three hours and then I've got to get back ... I have got to get back ... don't ask me why ... I have got to get back' (participant two, 71 years).

Furthermore, older women who have experienced domestic abuse at an earlier time in their life and which may remain unresolved in later life may also experience a number of emotional issues relating to their experiences such as frustration, anger, helplessness, hopelessness and low self-esteem. Many older women in the present study encountered these feelings and in many instances were unable to disclose this to others.

'It affects you in a horrible way ... , you feel worthless, you feel useless, and you feel like you don't get anything right ... your confidence and your self-esteem ... you don't have any ... and it affects you on many levels ... many levels' (participant one, 63 years).

'And your self-esteem ... and you just feel that you are totally and utterly stripped of any identity, so it is like building another self when you finally get away' (participant four, 76 years).

Effect on Relationships

Moreover, participants in the present study also spoke of the effect of the consequences of abuse on family relationships, particularly in terms of relationships with their children. This is a particularly important issue, especially in later life where family support may be most needed.

'Well ... my daughter was oldest and is mentally scarred, she will never ever live forward [her daughter dwells on the past events she has witnessed and finds it hard to be positive in terms of her life and relationships, especially emotional relationships] ... I mean my son was only two and a half so can only remember vaguely' (participant seven, 75 years).

'I find peace [names a place she visits with daughter]. I think my daughter knows it all ... I don't know. She feels the same ... I said to her, do you know ... I said ... you are a different person, and she said yeah and you are mum' (participant two, 71 years).

Giving Permission

A number of barriers in the reporting of domestic abuse by older women have been highlighted. In the present study, for example, participants spoke of how historically the home was perceived as private and 'what went on there was behind closed doors'. Participants also felt a sense of shame or embarrassment and as such kept their experiences 'hidden' from family, friends and neighbours.

'It was behind doors a lot, you know what I mean, like mine was, and in them days, years ago, there was nothing at all for us to turn to, you know' (participant eight, 76 years).

'No, I kept it [the abuse] to myself. Nobody understands why you keep it quiet and make excuses, but you're embarrassed and you love him' (participant 11, 66 years). Moreover, participants also spoke of the absence of formal or informal networks of potential support.

'There was nothing for you ... and my parents would say "you make your bed then lay there" really ... so I got no support ... so I think that is the problem and which made me accept the abuse in a very funny kind of a way' (participant one, 63 years).

'No refuges or whatever, not in those days, that's what I'm saying. You couldn't say to someone "please take me", there just wasn't anywhere to go' (participant two, 71 years).

'There was no point in calling the police, they would come and he would be in the cells and the next morning home again and I'd get it for reporting it' (participant eight, 76 years).

The feelings of shame or embarrassment experienced by women during their experiences of abuse often pervaded into later life. In the present study, for example, one participant spoke of how she felt unable to speak directly to her GP [general practitioner (doctor)] about her experiences, but rather handed him a note explaining her situation. Another participant spoke of how she felt that older women needed to be 'given permission' to speak out and to understand that it was acceptable to disclose domestic abuse.

We've got to give permission or try to get older women to realise that it is very wrong that they have been abused.

'So I wrote a little note [about previous domestic abuse] and went to see my GP. Gave him this note. I just put that I feel rather low, and wonder if counselling would help. And he looked at me and said "um . . . yes" (participant five, 64 years).

'I think it is the "hiddenness" of it that is the problem actually, a big part of it I think that needs to stop . . . I think we've got to give permission or try to get older women to realise that it is very wrong that they have been abused' (participant one, 63 years).

The Information Vacuum

From a contemporary perspective there is little evidence from the UK about access to services for older women. However, an American study has identified that older women are not always aware of the existence of services. This was echoed by older women in the present study who found out about services indirectly or felt that the services available would not meet their particular needs. For example, they felt that the focus was towards younger women with children.

'I just think there should be more information. I was very grateful to pick up this leaflet [local counselling service for older women], there again, it was in a mental health waiting room rather than a doctor's surgery. It was for older women and that was the only advert that I have ever seen. Most of it [domestic abuse services] applies to the young age groups because you just wouldn't go there as a person over 50. I still don't know whether it is just help and support for younger women with younger children ... there should be more out there and people made aware of the needs of older women' (participant five, 64 years).

To date there has been little exploration of the particular situation and specific health needs of older women.

'I don't know ... just I just couldn't cope last year ... I was crying all the time. I went to [names venue], there was a woman there ... she was a nurse and she said to me have some counselling ... honestly, it was the best thing. It really, really helped me' (participant 16, 63 years).

'I didn't talk about it [domestic abuse] to anyone and I was sitting on the bus [recently] and there was an advert for counselling [for domestic abuse]—have you this and that? And I thought that's me, and here we are' (participant ten, 64 years).

More Support for Older Abused Women

It is recognised that this was a small-scale study, which raises questions about the generalisability of the findings. However, the aim was not to make empirical generalisations but to explore older women's experiences of domestic abuse and as such the study achieved its aims.

As this study illustrated, to date there has been little exploration of the particular situation and specific health needs of older women in the UK who have experienced domestic abuse. Some of the reasons for this omission have been articulated and include a number of barriers to disclosure.

The specific effect of domestic abuse on older women has been identified as encompassing a number of factors, including long-term trauma alongside mental health problems: for example, depression, anxiety and other mental health issues, increased morbidity and mortality and the subsequent long-term consequences on family relationships and services.

Nurses and the wider health community can identify domestic abuse and understand the particular experiences and needs of older women affected by domestic abuse. Ultimately, it is crucial that services that are responsive to the needs of older women are developed effectively.

No Secrets

The policy in this field to date has largely focused on abuse of older women in the context of the No Secrets guidance. No Secrets provides guidance to professional agencies on the development and implementation of policies and procedures to protect vulnerable adults. In No Secrets domestic abuse is subsumed in vulnerable adult protection and as such it may be argued that the emphasis is on formal rather than domestic circumstances. Moreover, the lack of conceptual clarity that exists in terms of the terminology used, for example, how 'vulnerable' is defined, lacks specific guidance to professionals. As such, [Imogen] Blood [in *Older Women and Domestic Violence*] argues that this 'narrow definition' of vulnerable could discourage older women from seeking the support of services.

The limited research that has been undertaken to date and the existing literature in this field highlight that domestic abuse exerts a significant effect on the health and lives of older women. For older women there are additional challenges in accessing services and receiving appropriate support. The health community as a whole can identify domestic abuse and understand the particular experiences and needs of older women affected by domestic abuse. As a starting point in the debate it has been suggested that health screening and targeting of services and support may be one way forward, although the evidence surrounding the effectiveness of screening in domestic abuse to date is not unequivocal. A pivotal part of this challenge lies in recognising that domestic abuse among older women is a substantial issue at an organisational and service level, and in developing services and support, which are largely absent, to meet the particular needs of this group.

Victims of Child Abuse Suffer Long-Term Consequences

Child Welfare Information Gateway

Child Welfare Information Gateway is a service of the Administration for Children, Youth, and Families of the US Department of Health and Human Services.

An estimated 905,000 children were victims of child abuse or neglect in 2006. While physical injuries may or may not be immediately visible, abuse and neglect can have consequences for children, families, and society that last lifetimes, if not generations.

The impact of child abuse and neglect is often discussed in terms of physical, psychological, behavioral, and societal consequences. In reality, however, it is impossible to separate them completely. Physical consequences, such as damage to a child's growing brain, can have psychological implications such as cognitive delays or emotional difficulties. Psychological problems often manifest as high-risk behaviors. Depression and anxiety, for example, may make a person more likely to smoke, abuse alcohol or illicit drugs, or overeat. High-risk behaviors, in turn, can lead to long-term physical health problems such as sexually transmitted diseases, cancer, and obesity. . . .

Not all abused and neglected children will experience long-term consequences. Outcomes of individual cases vary widely and are affected by a combination of factors, including:

- The child's age and developmental status when the abuse or neglect occurred

- The type of abuse (physical abuse, neglect, sexual abuse, etc.)

- The frequency, duration, and severity of abuse

- The relationship between the victim and his or her abuser

The long-term impact of child abuse and neglect on physical health is just beginning to be explored.

Researchers also have begun to explore why, given similar conditions, some children experience long-term consequences of abuse and neglect while others emerge relatively unscathed. The ability to cope, and even thrive, following a negative experience is sometimes referred to as "resilience." A number of protective and promotive factors may contribute to an abused or neglected child's resilience. These include individual characteristics, such as optimism, self-esteem, intelligence, creativity, humor, and independence, as well as the acceptance of peers and positive individual influences such as teachers, mentors, and role models. Other factors can include the child's social environment and the family's access to social supports. Community well-being, including neighborhood stability and access to safe schools and adequate health care, are other protective and promotive factors.

Physical Health Consequences

The immediate physical effects of abuse or neglect can be relatively minor (bruises or cuts) or severe (broken bones, hemorrhage, or even death). In some cases the physical effects are temporary; however, the pain and suffering they cause a child should not be discounted. Meanwhile, the long-term impact of child abuse and neglect on physical health is just beginning to be explored. According to the National Survey of Child and Adolescent Well-Being (NSCAW), more than one-quarter of children who had been in foster care for longer than 12 months had some lasting or recurring health problem. Below are some outcomes researchers have identified:

Shaken baby syndrome. Shaking a baby is a common form of child abuse. The injuries caused by shaking a baby may not be immediately noticeable and may include bleeding in the eye or brain, damage to the spinal cord and neck, and rib or bone fractures.

Impaired brain development. Child abuse and neglect have been shown, in some cases, to cause important regions of the brain to fail to form or grow properly, resulting in impaired development. These alterations in brain maturation have long-term consequences for cognitive, language, and academic abilities. NSCAW found more than three-quarters of foster children between 1 and 2 years of age to be at medium to high risk for problems with brain development, as opposed to less than half of children in a control sample.

Poor physical health. Several studies have shown a relationship between various forms of household dysfunction (including childhood abuse) and poor health. Adults who experienced abuse or neglect during childhood are more likely to suffer from physical ailments such as allergies, arthritis, asthma, bronchitis, high blood pressure, and ulcers.

Psychological Consequences

The immediate emotional effects of abuse and neglect—isolation, fear, and an inability to trust—can translate into lifelong consequences, including low self-esteem, depression, and relationship difficulties. Researchers have identified links between child abuse and neglect and the following:

Difficulties during infancy. Depression and withdrawal symptoms were common among children as young as 3 who experienced emotional, physical, or environmental neglect.

Poor mental and emotional health. In one long-term study, as many as 80 percent of young adults who had been abused met the diagnostic criteria for at least one psychiatric disorder at age 21. These young adults exhibited many problems, including depression, anxiety, eating disorders, and suicide attempts. Other psychological and emotional conditions associated with abuse and neglect include panic disorder, dissociative disorders, attention-deficit/hyperactivity disorder, depression, anger, posttraumatic stress disorder, and reactive attachment disorder.

Cognitive difficulties. NSCAW found that children placed in out-of-home care due to abuse or neglect tended to score lower than the general population on measures of cognitive capacity, language development, and academic achievement. A 1999 LONGSCAN [Longitudinal Studies of Child Abuse and Neglect] study also found a relationship between substantiated child maltreatment and poor academic performance and classroom functioning for school-age children.

Social difficulties. Children who experience rejection or neglect are more likely to develop antisocial traits as they grow up. Parental neglect is also associated with borderline personality disorders and violent behavior.

Behavioral Consequences

Not all victims of child abuse and neglect will experience behavioral consequences. However, behavioral problems appear to be more likely among this group, even at a young age. An NSCAW survey of children ages 3 to 5 in foster care found these children displayed clinical or borderline levels of behavioral problems at a rate more than twice that of the general population. Later in life, child abuse and neglect appear to make the following more likely:

Difficulties during adolescence. Studies have found abused and neglected children to be at least 25 percent more likely to experience problems such as delinquency, teen pregnancy, low academic achievement, drug use, and mental health problems. Other studies suggest that abused or neglected children are

more likely to engage in sexual risk-taking as they r
lescence, thereby increasing their chances of con............
sexually transmitted disease.

Approximately one-third of abused and neglected children will eventually victimize their own children.

Juvenile delinquency and adult criminality. According to a National Institute of Justice study, abused and neglected children were 11 times more likely to be arrested for criminal behavior as a juvenile, 2.7 times more likely to be arrested for violent and criminal behavior as an adult, and 3.1 times more likely to be arrested for one of many forms of violent crime (juvenile or adult).

Alcohol and other drug abuse. Research consistently reflects an increased likelihood that abused and neglected children will smoke cigarettes, abuse alcohol, or take illicit drugs during their lifetime. According to a report from the National Institute on Drug Abuse, as many as two-thirds of people in drug treatment programs reported being abused as children.

Abusive behavior. Abusive parents often have experienced abuse during their own childhoods. It is estimated approximately one-third of abused and neglected children will eventually victimize their own children.

Societal Consequences

While child abuse and neglect almost always occur within the family, the impact does not end there. Society as a whole pays a price for child abuse and neglect, in terms of both direct and indirect costs.

Direct costs. Direct costs include those associated with maintaining a child welfare system to investigate and respond to allegations of child abuse and neglect, as well as expenditures by the judicial, law enforcement, health, and mental health systems. A 2001 report by Prevent Child Abuse America estimates these costs at $24 billion per year.

Indirect costs. Indirect costs represent the long-term economic consequences of child abuse and neglect. These include costs associated with juvenile and adult criminal activity, mental illness, substance abuse, and domestic violence. They can also include loss of productivity due to unemployment and underemployment, the cost of special education services, and increased use of the health care system. Prevent Child Abuse America estimated these costs at more than $69 billion per year.

Child Abuse Impacts Society

Much research has been done about the possible consequences of child abuse and neglect. The effects vary depending on the circumstances of the abuse or neglect, personal characteristics of the child, and the child's environment. Consequences may be mild or severe; disappear after a short period or last a lifetime; and affect the child physically, psychologically, behaviorally, or in some combination of all three ways.

Ultimately, due to related costs to public entities such as the health care, human services, and educational systems, abuse and neglect impact not just the child and family, but society as a whole.

Organizations to Contact

The editors have compiled the following list of organizations concerned with the issues debated in this book. The descriptions are derived from materials provided by the organizations. All have publications or information available for interested readers. The list was compiled on the date of publication of the present volume; the information provided here may change. Be aware that many organizations take several weeks or longer to respond to inquiries, so allow as much time as possible.

American Bar Association Commission on Domestic & Sexual Violence
740 Fifteenth St. NW, Washington, DC   20005-1019
(202) 662-1000 • fax: (202) 662-1594
website: www.americanbar.org/groups/domestic_violence.html

The American Bar Association's Commission on Domestic & Sexual Violence provides ongoing education, publications, and technical assistance to attorneys representing victims of domestic violence and sexual assault.

Childhelp
15757 N. Seventy-Eighth St., Ste. B, Scottsdale, AZ   85260
(480) 922-8212 • fax: (480) 922-7061
website: www.childhelp.org

Childhelp works to help prevent and treat child abuse. The organization provides residential care and counseling services for abused and neglected children through its group and foster homes. It promotes public awareness of child abuse issues and offers a child abuse hotline that services North America. Its publications include *Child Abuse and You* and the *Child Help Newsletter.*

Child Welfare Information Gateway
Children's Bureau/ACYF, 1250 Maryland Ave. SW, 8th Fl.
Washington, DC   20024

(800) 394-3366

website: www.childwelfare.gov

The Child Welfare Information Gateway, which was formed by the merger of the National Clearinghouse on Child Abuse and Neglect Information and the National Adoption Information Clearinghouse, is run by the US Department of Health and Human Service's Children's Bureau in the Administration for Children, Youth, and Families. The organization publishes fact sheets, issues briefs, and reports on its website, and provides other resources on child welfare and adoption.

Emerge: Counseling and Education to Stop Domestic Violence

2464 Massachusetts Ave., Ste. 101, Cambridge, MA   02140

(617) 547-9879 • fax: (617) 547-0904

website: www.emergedv.com

The mission of Emerge is to eliminate violence in intimate relationships. The organization provides a variety of counseling services, training workshops, anger management courses, and parenting seminars for therapists and counselors as well as batterers. Among the videos, books, articles, and manuals published by the organization are *Why Do They Kill? Men Who Murder Their Intimate Partners* and "Treatment Programs for Batterers."

FaithTrust Institute

2900 Eastlake Ave. East, Ste. 200, Seattle, WA   98102

(206) 634-1903 • fax: (206) 634-0115

website: www.faithtrustinstitute.org

FaithTrust Institute is an interfaith training and education organization whose purpose is to end domestic and sexual violence. The group provides support and educational resources to religious organizations in their efforts to encourage healthy family relationships and eliminate sexual and domestic violence.

Family Research Laboratory (FRL)
University of New Hampshire
126 Horton Social Science Center
Durham, NH   03824-3586
(603) 862-1888 • fax: (603) 862-1122
website: www.unh.edu/frl

Since 1975, the Family Research Laboratory has devoted itself to understanding the causes and consequences of family violence and working to dispel myths about family violence through public education. The organization publishes numerous books and articles on the physical abuse of children, the physical abuse of intimate partners, marital rape, corporal punishment, pornography, and verbal aggression.

Futures Without Violence
100 Montgomery St., The Presidio, San Francisco, CA   94129
(415) 678-5500 • fax: (415) 529-2930
website: www.endabuse.org

Futures Without Violence, formerly Family Violence Prevention Fund, works to prevent and end violence against women and children around the world. The organization publishes brochures, action kits, books, and general information packets on domestic violence.

Institute for Family Violence Studies
Florida State University, 296 Champion Way
University Center Bldg. C 2306, Tallahassee, FL   32306-2570
(850) 644-6303
website: www.familyvio.csw.fsu.edu

Florida State University's Institute for Family Violence Studies conducts research on family violence and gender discrimination, provides training for industry professionals and advocates, and conducts online tutorials for the study of domestic violence issues.

National Coalition Against Domestic Violence (NCADV)
1 Broadway, Ste. B-210, Denver, CO   80203
(303) 839-1852 • fax: (303) 831-9251
website: www.ncadv.org

NCADV was formed in 1978 and became the largest US coalition of grassroots shelter programs and services for battered women and their children. The organization provides technical help and education to family violence professionals, it advocates for public policy and legislation, and it sponsors national conferences that bring together experts in family violence policy, law, and services.

National Coalition of Anti-Violence Programs (NCAVP)

240 W. Thirty-Fifth St., Ste. 200, New York, NY   10001
(212) 714-1184 • fax: (212) 714-2627
e-mail: info@ncavp.org
website: www.ncavp.org

The NCAVP is a nationwide network of organizations that address the problem of violence in and against the lesbian/gay/transgendered/bisexual/HIV-AIDS-afflicted (LGTBH) community, including intimate partner violence. The coalition publishes annual reports on LGTBH domestic violence and hate crimes and publishes media releases throughout the year.

Safe Horizon

2 Lafayette St., 3rd Fl., New York, NY   10007
(212) 577-7700 • fax: (212) 577-3897
website: www.safehorizon.org

The mission of Safe Horizon is to provide support, prevent violence, and promote justice for victims, their families, and communities. The organization provides shelters, counseling services, and hotlines for victims of domestic violence and child abuse. Safe Horizon also raises awareness of issues of violence and abuse and its impact on the home, the workplace, and communities.

Bibliography

Books

R. Lundy
Bancroft et al.
The Batterer as Parent: Addressing the Impact of Domestic Violence on Family Dynamics. 2nd ed. Thousand Oaks, CA: Sage, 2012.

Ola W. Barnett et al.
Family Violence Across the Lifespan: An Introduction. Thousand Oaks, CA: Sage, 2011.

Lisa M. Conradi and Robert Geffner, eds.
Female Offenders of Intimate Partner Violence: Current Controversies, Research and Treatment Approaches. New York: Routledge, 2012.

Cynthia Crosson-Tower
Understanding Child Abuse and Neglect. 8th ed. Englewood Cliffs, NJ: Prentice-Hall, 2009.

Anisha Durve
The Power to Break Free: Surviving Domestic Violence, with a Special Reference to Abuse in Indian Marriages. Cleveland: Power Press, 2012.

Sandra A. Graham-Bermann and Alytia A. Levendosky, eds.
How Intimate Partner Violence Affects Children: Developmental Research, Case Studies, and Evidence-Based Intervention. Washington, DC: American Psychological Association, 2011.

Janice Haaken
Hard Knocks: Domestic Violence and the Psychology of Storytelling. New York: Routledge, 2010.

John Hamel, ed.   *Intimate Partner and Family Abuse: A Casebook of Gender Inclusive Therapy.* New York: Springer, 2008.

Angela J. Hattery and Earl Smith   *The Social Dynamics of Family Violence.* Boulder, CO: Westview, 2012.

Peter Lehmann and Catherine Simmons   *Strengths-Based Batterer Intervention: A New Paradigm in Ending Family Violence.* New York: Springer, 2009.

Sonya B. Norman et al.   *Drinking Among Female Victims of Intimate Partner Violence: Mechanisms and Intervention.* Hauppauge, NY: Nova Science, 2011.

Brian K. Payne and Randy R. Gainey   *Family Violence and Criminal Justice: A Life-Course Approach.* New Providence, NJ: LexisNexis/Matthew Bender, 2009.

Janice L. Ristock, ed.   *Intimate Partner Violence in LGBTQ Lives.* New York: Routledge, 2011.

Diane S. Sandell and Lois Hudson   *Ending Elder Abuse: A Family Guide.* Fort Bragg, CA: Cypress House, 2010.

Lita Linzer Schwartz and Natalie K. Isser   *Endangered Children, Homicide and Other Crimes.* 2nd ed. Boca Raton, FL: CRC Press, 2012.

Periodicals

Nicholas Bakalar   "Child Abuse Investigations Didn't Reduce Risk, a Study Finds," *New York Times*, October 11, 2010.

Philip Bulman   "Elder Abuse Emerges from the
                       Shadows of Public Consciousness,"
                       NIJ Journal, April 2010.
                       www.ncjrs.gov.

James J.   "Understanding the Impact of
Colangelo and   Childhood Sexual Abuse on Women's
Kathleen   Sexuality," *Journal of Mental Health*
Keefe-Cooperman   *Counseling*, January 2012.

Community Care   "A Culture of Complicity," March 31,
                       2011.

Martha Coulter   "Reducing Domestic Violence and
and Carla   Other Criminal Recidivism:
VandeWeerd   Effectiveness of a Multilevel Batterers
                       Intervention Program," *Violence and*
                       Victims, November 2, 2009.

Corrie Cutrer   "When Someone You Love Is Abused:
                       What You Need to Know and How
                       You Can Make a Difference," *Today's*
                       Christian Woman, May–June 2009.

Kathryn E.   "Influence of Heavy Episodic
Gallagher and   Drinking on the Relation Between
Dominic J.   Men's Locus of Control and
Parrott   Aggression Toward Intimate
                       Partners," *Journal of Studies on*
                       Alcohol and Drugs, March 2010.

Lisa Gibbs and   "Elder Abuse: A Medical Perspective,"
Laura Mosqueda   *Aging Health*, December 2010.

Mark Hanson "Unsettling Science: After Decades of Prosecuting Suspect Infant Deaths, Experts Are Still Debating Whether Shaken Baby Syndrome Exists," *ABA Journal*, December 2011.

Susan Heitler "Three of a Kind: Dictatorship, Terrorism, and Domestic Violence," *Psychology Today*, September 10, 2011.

C.J. Hildreth "Elder Abuse," *JAMA: The Journal of the American Medical Association*, August 3, 2011.

Sabatina James "How I Escaped," *Newsweek*, March 12, 2012.

Mary Ann Moon "Violence Raises Women's Risk of Mental Disorders," *Clinical Psychiatry News*, November 2011.

Thomas D. Morton and Lisa Reese "Domestic Violence, the Recession and Child Welfare," *Policy & Practice*, April 2011.

Neil Osterweil "Child-to-Parent Violence Common in Court Records," *Clinical Psychiatry News*, December 2011.

Sheetal Ranjan and Chitra Raghavan "The Economic Recession and Intimate Partner Violence: Imbalances in the Traditional Roles of Men and Women Can Put Women at Risk of Violence from Men, and the Current Recession Is Exacerbating This Risk," *Journal of Employee Assistance*, April 2010.

Patricia Sheehan   "Elder Abuse, Zero Tolerance: Recognizing and Responding to Abuse, Neglect and Exploitation," *Long-Term Living*, June 2011.

Gina Stepp   "Family Violence," *Vision*, Winter 2010.

Gretchen Voss   "'I Was Forced to Get Pregnant,'" *Redbook*, July 2011.

Liz Welch   "Three Generations of Domestic Violence Stop Here," *Glamour*, November 2009.

Index

A

Acquired immune deficiency syndrome (AIDS), 77

Ad Hoc Working Group on Women, Mental Health, Mental Illness, and Addictions, 71–75

Adult criminality, 199

Afghanistan, 51

African Americans
  domestic violence, 117, 154, 155
  gender-based violence, 76–79

Aggression
  decrease in, 147
  gender differences in, 149
  of jihad, 37
  as modality, 45
  physical, 178
  prosecution of, 157–158
  reasons for, 59, 148, 165

Alcohol and other drug abuse (AODA). *See* Alcohol use/abuse; Substance abuse

Alcohol or other drugs (AOD), 25–28, 167

Alcohol use/abuse
  binge drinking, 25
  with child abuse, 71–74, 162, 195, 199
  child risk of, 163–168
  domestic violence and, 65, 67
  gender differences with, 70
  health care costs with, 173
  intimate partner violence and, 24, 25, 63
  overview, 163–165

treatment for, 148
violence against men and, 150
violence against women and, 21–22

American Association of Retired People (magazine), 86

American Journal of Public Health (magazine), 58–59

Antisocial behavior/personality, 71, 88, 165, 198

Anxiety
  acute, 188
  child abuse and, 195, 198
  disorders, 71, 72, 188
  domestic violence and, 22, 192
  intimate partner violence and, 23, 24

Archdiocesan Committee on Domestic Violence, 119

Archer, J., 81

Arrests
  with alcohol abuse, 70
  for assault, 43
  for domestic violence, 66, 68–69
  gender differences with, 67, 68–69
  for home break-ins, 53
  mandatory arrest laws, 65, 77, 148, 154–156, 158
  pro-arrest policy, 65

Ash Institute for Democratic Governance and Innovation, 113

Asian Americans, 117

Astor, Brooke, 16

M

N

T

U

V